"This entertaining volume presents Thomas Aquinas, the renowned Dominican saint-scholar, discussing the practice of lot-drawing and similar ventures of chance. Thomas affirms that such gambling can be appropriate in practical matters where moral certainty cannot be reached otherwise. These reflections are now put before us in Father Peter Carey's lucid English translation of Thomas's text, helpfully supplemented with brief essays by other esteemed Thomas scholars. Readers will enjoy and benefit from this work."

—Bruce Williams
OP, Pontifical Angelicum University, Rome

"Among the many wordy and warring interpreters of our faith, Thomas Aquinas is distinguished by the sweet thoroughness of his calm and broad reason. This letter to a friend on 'the casting of lots' is a wonderful oasis of broad and grounded clarity, and helpfully accompanied by insightful essays from Anglican authors on Scripture, tradition, and reason. Treat yourself in this harried time, and consider the Holy Spirit when next you flip a coin."

—Rebecca Lyman
The Church Divinity School of the Pacific

"If grace perfects nature, then the guidance of the Holy Spirit exceeds without overriding our best shared practices of discernment. This is the wisdom of Thomas's lovely treatise on casting lots— reading omens and stars, drawing 'straws,' rolling dice. Carey's translation and commentary, along with brief essays by eminent scholars, make this an ideal introduction to an 'Anglican' Thomas."

—Anthony D. Baker
Seminary of the Southwest

"Thomas Aquinas is the greatest of all medieval theologians. If that fact alone has kept you till now from attempting to read his work, I highly recommend that you begin with Peter Carey's translation of *De Sortibus: A Letter to a Friend about the Casting of Lots*, in which Saint Thomas shows himself to be humane, imaginative, fanciful, and at times even humorous and romantic. Enter the Middle Ages by a door you didn't even know was there—and have fun."

—**Thomas Cahill**
Author of *Mysteries of the Middle Ages*

"Peter Carey's *De Sortibus*, produced during the dark days of the pandemic, is like a flowering plant miraculously appearing in a crevice of a concrete wasteland. What a pleasure to read this formerly untranslated letter by Thomas Aquinas and its accompanying essays by Anglican and Roman scholars. It reminds me as an Anglican committed to the ecumenical vision how much Aquinas has to offer that vision with his comprehensive use of biblical, patristic, and classical sources accompanied by his balanced and reasonable approach to the matter in hand. Aquinas truly belongs to the whole Christian family. May they all be one."

—**Andrew R. St. John**
St. Thomas Church Fifth Avenue, New York

"Peter Carey has done us a great service in translating this short work by Aquinas. The expert commentaries included alongside the translation light up Aquinas's gem of a text and remind us that we still have much to learn from the Angelic Doctor, even in his littlest writings. I warmly commend this wonderful edition of *De Sortibus* to newcomers and seasoned readers of Aquinas alike."

—**Nathan Lyons**
University of Notre Dame, Australia

"Thomas Aquinas's works, like his reputation, can be daunting. But if you'd like to find a good place to start, you can find no better place to begin than with Peter Carey's delightful translation of *De Sortibus*."

—**Mark Larrimore**
The New School, New York

"Peter Carey's translation of *De Sortibus: A Letter to a Friend about the Casting of Lots* reveals Aquinas's keen skill in the art of discernment. The book sheds light on an ancient form of divination, itself rendered an appropriate tool for discernment in a variety of circumstances. If you wish to learn more about Aquinas's pastoral sensitivity and theological acuity—and how these are woven together for the good of Christian community—read this book!"

—**Amy Bentley Lamborn**
The University of the South, Sewanee

De Sortibus

01.11.22

For Stephen
From Peter

May the coming year be
a year of grace for us.

De Sortibus

A Letter to a Friend about the Casting of Lots

BY

—SAINT THOMAS AQUINAS—

TRANSLATED BY
PETER CAREY

EDITED BY JANE SHANNON

FOREWORD BY ANDREW DAVISON

 CASCADE *Books* · Eugene, Oregon

DE SORTIBUS
A Letter to a Friend about the Casting of Lots

Cascade Books
An Imprint of Wipf and Stock Publishers
199 W. 8th Ave., Suite 3
Eugene, OR 97401

www.wipfandstock.com

PAPERBACK ISBN: 978-1-7252-8976-5
HARDCOVER ISBN: 978-1-7252-8977-2
EBOOK ISBN: 978-1-7252-8978-9

Cataloging-in-Publication data:

Names: Thomas, Aquinas, Saint, 1225?–1274, author. | Carey, Peter, translator

Title: De sortibus : a letter to a friend about the casting of lots / by Saint Thomas Aquinas ; translated and introduced by Peter Carey.

Description: Eugene, OR : Cascade Books, 2021 | Includes bibliographical references.

Identifiers: ISBN 978-1-7252-8976-5 (paperback) | ISBN 978-1-7252-8977-2 (hardcover) | ISBN 978-1-7252-8978-9 (ebook)

Subjects: LCSH: Thomas, Aquinas, Saint, 1225?–1274. | Thomas, Aquinas, Saint, 1225?–1274—De sortibus. | Choice by lots—History. | Philosophy, Medieval. | Divinization.

Classification: LCC B765.T54 C37 2021 (print) | LCC B765.T54 (ebook)

01/04/21

Cover image: the portrait of Saint Thomas Aquinas was painted by Tobias Haller, also an essay contributor in this book, and it is printed here with his permission.

Dedicated to
Saint Thomas Aquinas:
a great teacher
who continues to teach us today

Contents

About the Author and Translator

Peter Carey was born in New York City in 1938. In 1959, he entered the Dominican Order, and in 1966, was ordained a priest.

After graduate work in Rome, he left the Dominicans, but remained in Rome, teaching English there for five more years. He returned to New York in 1977. He worked first for Price Waterhouse where he fine-tuned his knowledge of translating technical material into plain English. Peter then worked for Citibank, becoming a vice president in 1987. In 1987, he also became an Episcopalian, and in 1990, because of the AIDS epidemic, he returned to the priesthood in the Episcopal Church.

In 1994, Peter was diagnosed with chronic myelogenous leukemia and nearly died, but in 2000, he was fortunate enough to be the recipient of one of the first genetically engineered cancer drugs, and fully recovered.

After thirty years of life together with his partner, David Natoli, the couple married in Canada in 2007 and received the Blessing of a Civil Marriage in New York that same year.

Carey served as vicar of St. Stephen's Episcopal Church in Woodlawn, New York, from 1991 to 1997, and from that time until the present, he has served as an assisting priest at the Church of the Holy Apostles in Manhattan, a parish noted for its service to the poor through the Holy Apostles Soup Kitchen. In 2016, he celebrated the fiftieth anniversary of ordination.

In 1992, Carey was named to the Board of Trustees of the Episcopal Diocese of New York where he served until 1997.

Peter has published two books of sermons, a history of his family, and numerous articles. At the start of the COVID-19 pandemic, he revived his interest in Saint Thomas Aquinas and re-translated into plain English his earlier translation of Aquinas's *De Sortibus,* which he calls *A Letter to a Friend about the Casting of Lots.* This work of the Angelic Doctor has never before been published in English.

Foreword

ANDREW DAVISON

Decisions can be difficult: difficult for individuals, and sometimes destructive for groups if they can't agree. Small wonder then, that people down the ages have looked for ways to have their choices made for them. In ancient Greece or Rome, you might seek guidance in the entrails of animals, Christians have tried it by opening the Bible at random, and in the Bible itself, people draw lots.

With characteristic warmth, Thomas Aquinas recognized the human impulse at work here, in his discussion of casting lots, *De Sortibus*. Today's reader may be surprised that Aquinas did not entirely rule out the casting of lots, but his reasons show his wisdom. Sometimes, nature can indeed tell us things about the future that we cannot sense ourselves. Birds and other animals can react to what is coming in ways we cannot. Or, Aquinas writes of civic affairs, it can sometimes be better to settle a worldly dispute by drawing lots than to continue to suffer the effects of ongoing dissent.

Nonetheless, generally speaking, his line leads us away from lots. Yes, choice can be difficult, but it is also part of what makes us human. There is a dignity to taking responsibility, and to taking the time we need to come to a good decision. The theological humanism of Aquinas is much on display here, celebrating our ability to think and to act: if you know what you should do, get on with it; if you don't, best to proceed by human *endeavor, prudence,* and *harmony of wills,* to get where you need to be.

Up until now, Thomas's often fascinating, even delightful, treatise on casting lots has been almost entirely neglected, and out of reach to readers without a command of Latin. Now no longer. Peter Carey has given us an excellent translation, making the text accessible for twenty-first-century readers. He has also provided an Introduction to tell the endearing story of how Aquinas came to write on this topic and assembled a remarkable collection of essays to help the reader understand its background: in the Scriptures, for instance, and the writings of the early church.

A notable number of these essays are by Anglican authors. The translation and the essays taken together therefore reflect the shape of Father Peter's life to date, stretching from his days as a Dominican friar, when he first turned to translating this text, to his home in the Episcopal Church and its priesthood later on. It is a tale, spanning Rome and New York, to which I think he would be happy to attach words from Psalm 16: "The lot is fallen unto me in a fair ground." The obvious delight with which the scholars gathered here have contributed to this marvelous project is also testament to that gift and esteem for friendship that Peter shares with Aquinas (and to which the writing of *De Sortibus* is itself a witness, as Peter's Introduction makes clear).

A key to understanding Aquinas is his saying from the *Summa theologiae* that "grace does not abolish nature, but perfects it." This is also the message of *De Sortibus,* as Thomas illustrates beautifully here how *human judgment* is enriched by the gifts of grace.

Few indeed are the subjects on which Thomas Aquinas does not have something sensible and illuminating to say. That is certainly true of *De Sortibus,* but its treasures have been closed for English readers up to now. Thanks to Peter Carey's beautiful translation, and its enlightening accompanying essays and information, it now stands open for us all.

Preface

Originally, I translated this work by Thomas Aquinas in 1963. What you hold in your hands now is a new, easier-to-read version of *De Sortibus*, a letter Thomas wrote to a friend on the casting of lots. Scholars agree he wrote the letter from Paris, but they disagree about whether it was in 1270 or 1271.

When I first translated this work, like Aquinas (albeit many centuries later), I was a member of the Order of Preachers, commonly known as the Dominicans, from 1959 to 1971. Let me share with you a few key events about how I originally translated this work as a young man in the process of becoming a Catholic priest, and then explain why I created this new translation as a retired Episcopal priest.

After an introductory year called the novitiate, the Dominicans require that students for the priesthood begin their intellectual formation by studying philosophy for three years. As young Dominican students, we drank deeply of the philosophy of our brother Thomas, while we also explored great thinkers, starting with Greek philosophers and ending with the dense, difficult writings of Martin Heidegger.

During the second year of philosophical studies, some students were given the opportunity to work toward a master's degree in philosophy, and I was chosen to be a candidate for that degree. We were required to maintain high grades in our courses, to write and defend a dissertation, and to pass a rigorous oral examination.

For my dissertation, I hoped to find a short work by Saint Thomas that had never before appeared in English. I eventually found this letter about casting lots in the last volume of a multi-volume edition of the complete works of Thomas Aquinas in Latin, published in Italy by Marietti in 1954.

My choice was unusual. The curriculum in any Dominican house of studies, then and now, is heavily weighted toward the study of Aquinas, and so most of my fellow students wanted to branch out. I, on the other hand, wanted to stay with Aquinas—he brought me into the Dominican Order in the first place. I loved the Dominican emphasis on study as a form of worship. As one of my fellow students put it, "I want to love God with my mind, not just my heart." I was also drawn to the order for its practice of choral liturgy, its emphasis on preaching, and its community life.

I approached Fr. Nicholas Halligan, a faculty member of St. Stephen's College, Dover, Massachusetts, where I was studying. He looked over *De Sortibus*, saw merit in my idea, and agreed to be my director.

Fr. Halligan came up with an ingenious way of getting me to complete the work in just a year. He directed me to appear in his office every Friday evening at 8 p.m. to turn in what I'd accomplished each week. He would then go over it with me, carefully correcting my syntax, and patiently pointing out my mistranslations.

When the translation was done, I then needed to write a short biography of Aquinas, a commentary, and a description of the historical context of the work. Then I was to note parallels with the themes of this work and those of Aquinas's other works. It was a big job.

When I finished, I was satisfied with my work, and apparently my examiners were also, because as a first-year student in theology, I was awarded my master's degree in philosophy. However, my translation didn't quite please me. It was too literal, too scholastic; the sentences were too long. The whole text adhered too closely to the Latin. It was, quite simply, dry.

In 1966, I was ordained a priest, and after one additional year of theological studies, I was asked to teach the history of philosophy at St. Stephen's. In August 1968, I was sent to Rome, to the University of Saint Thomas, known as the Angelicum, for post-graduate work in moral theology, my chosen field.

By January 1971, I had completed all the requirements to receive my doctorate, but I hesitated to take the final step. This is to take a public oath to uphold the teachings of the Catholic Church, including its moral teaching. I had doubts about certain teachings stated at the time by the papal magisterium.

It was a period of considerable change in the Catholic Church. In the aftermath of the Second Vatican Council, I felt unable to swear to uphold certain doctrines that many theologians were questioning, about which I had doubts, and which were not permanent or universally meaningful or binding. So I asked for, and was given, permission to live outside the Dominican Order. Later, I petitioned the Pope, and received permission to leave the Dominicans, as well as a dispensation from the duties of the priesthood.

After I left the Dominicans, I began a new life: I found a wonderful apartment in the famous Trastevere quarter of Rome, and I found a job I loved: teaching English as a Second Language.

During this transition, I was fortunate to have a colleague who worked in educational publishing before we met in Rome. She taught me how to write about highly technical information in a way that people can more easily understand. At that time, a few organizations were beginning to use this technique called "plain English" to create consumer agreements and even contracts, so that more people could actually understand them.

The techniques of plain English include writing more in active voice than passive; using contractions for a conversational tone; and editing for shorter sentences, shorter paragraphs, and shorter words. Sentence fragments? Fine.

By 1977, armed with my teaching experience and my ability to write in plain English, I returned to New York City where I quickly found work. First, I translated documents written in legal language, such as credit applications and pension plan explanations, into more readable communications. After a few years, I found my dream job: I worked at Citibank as a business writer specializing in banking, traveling all over the world to research and write about the bank's activities—in plain English. In 1987, I was promoted to vice president.

Then something happened that changed my life—the AIDS epidemic.

By 1981, when the AIDS epidemic hit New York City, I was attending an Episcopal Church; I then began to feel I should return to the active priesthood—this time in the Episcopal Church.

I saw the need for priests who could care spiritually for the sick, bury the dead, and console their partners and families. In 1990, I was received as a priest in the Episcopal Church and served until my "retirement" in 2000.

As a retiree, I have continued to work as an assisting priest at the Church of the Holy Apostles in New York City, famous for its Soup Kitchen that feeds more than a thousand people a day, five days a week.

Throughout this time, resting on a shelf was *De Sortibus*.

When Covid-19 arrived, and I was sheltering at home, I dug out my old translation of *De Sortibus* and began to re-translate it anew. That proved the perfect task to get my mind off both politics and the anxiety of the second epidemic that had arrived, unwanted, into my life. My goal was to make it easier for readers to understand how Thomas Aquinas thought, and to share his wisdom with a broader audience.

I have tried in this translation to give readers insight into Thomas Aquinas's thinking: to see how his theology reflected the interests of his own time; to explore some of the great themes of his philosophy and theology; and then to observe how Aquinas's thoughts about God and humanity were illustrated by a specific topic, a rather unusual one.

As a young man, I was strongly drawn to this great thinker, Saint Thomas Aquinas. As an old man, my respect and love for the Doctor whom the church has commended to so many through the ages, has endured. I hope you will gain insights and wisdom from his wise words, too.

—*Peter Carey*

Acknowledgments

In 1996 the then First Lady Hillary Clinton wrote a book called *It Takes a Village*. The idea of Mrs. Clinton's book was that individuals and groups have an important impact on children as they grow up. I've discovered that that same idea is true when you write a book, at least the kind of book that I've written: you need the help of both groups and individuals to get the job done. Now that this book is finished, the time has come for me to thank those groups and individuals who helped, and it's a great pleasure for me to do so.

There is no doubt that the person who helped me most, in life and in my work, has been my husband David Natoli. We met in 1976; we married when we were able legally to do so in 2007; and for nearly forty-five years David has been at my side encouraging and supporting me. What a gift he has been.

Before David, there was a group that also gave me much, and that group was the Dominican Order. I was a Dominican from 1959 until 1971. From that religious order, formally known as the Order of Preachers, I learned to love God, not only with my heart and my emotions, but also with my mind.

The Order taught me that study can be understood as a kind of worship and that good preaching and good teaching go together. Most of all they taught me to love the writings of one of their greatest sons—Saint Thomas Aquinas, who was perhaps one of the most profound thinkers and certainly one of the most prodigious writers the world has ever known. This book is my tribute to Saint

Thomas and to the Order to which we both belonged, even though we were separated in time by almost seven hundred years.

The next group I need to thank is the Episcopal Church, that constituent part of the Anglican Communion, which, in my understanding, is a branch of the one, holy, catholic, and apostolic church.

In the Episcopal Church I found everything I knew I needed as a Christian—the sacraments, the Scriptures, community life, and common prayer. I found a church where power is shared and where freedom and reason and common sense prevail; a church where study and the intellectual life are valued and where the gospel is preached—and preached well.

Like Saint Thomas, the Episcopal Church is not at war with the world around it but understands the world as fundamentally good and seeks to harmonize its best values with the Christian tradition and with the gospel. For all these reasons, and more, I am grateful to the Episcopal Church for having received me as a priest in 1990, and I thank the church from the bottom of my heart for the opportunity to preach the gospel from its pulpits and to lead the Eucharist from its altars.

Now I turn to the individuals who contributed so much toward helping me publish for the very first time in English, this previously unknown but fascinating work of Thomas Aquinas— *De Sortibus,* and subtitled by me, *A Letter to a Friend about the Casting of Lots.*

The coda I have added to the Latin title of Saint Thomas's *De Sortibus* is appropriate for two reasons. The first is that this *opusculum,* or short work, is a letter. The second reason is that all of the individuals who helped with this book are personal friends and having had friends to work with on this project has been a joy. I'm so grateful to them for their help and friendship.

The first person I need to mention, after David, is Anthony Valentino. He is the person who keeps our house running and our spirits high. Without him, there would be no book. From helping me with the computer files to getting us to our doctor visits, he's the man who makes it all happen.

Another indispensable assistant was the editor of this book, Jane Shannon. I've known Jane, who is now semi-retired, since our days working together at Citibank, where she headed a large department of writers, editors, and designers. I don't know of any better editor.

Then there were the distinguished contributors to this volume. Each from her or his own perspective has helped the potential readers of this letter to understand Saint Thomas better. They are Andrew Davison, Matthew Fox, Deirdre Good, Tobias Haller, Boniface Ramsey, and Christopher Wells. To learn more about these outstanding scholars, I refer you to the "Biographies of the Essay Contributors" section of this book.

I must also not fail to mention the indispensable help of Thomas O'Meara, one of the Dominican Order's most distinguished scholars on Aquinas. Tom read my translation of *De Sortibus* and corrected its errors. I thank him heartily for placing his mastery of medieval Latin at the service of this translation.

When I first translated *De Sortibus* in 1963, I was young and in good health. Now I am old and no longer in good health, but I have been kept in good enough shape in recent years with the help of the amazing doctors, nurses, and technicians of Memorial Sloan Kettering Cancer Center in New York City. They have kept me going. I need to mention two doctors in particular: Peter Maslak, MD, and Howard Weinstein, MD. Without them, there would have been no *De Sortibus* in English.

There are also some Episcopal priests and an Episcopal bishop who over the years befriended David and me and nourished us spiritually. They are Bishop Andrew St. John, and the Reverends Anna Pearson, Elizabeth Maxwell, John-David Van Dooren, and William Greenlaw. Each one an outstanding priest and a faithful friend.

Finally, I need to mention the friends who pitched in at critical moments to assist and encourage. An expert in the field of computers, Chad Rancourt, was invariably one of the most helpful and certainly one of the kindest.

Acknowledgments

Most of all, my thanks need to go to Saint Thomas Aquinas himself. He greatly enriched my life. How could I fail to thank the Angelic Doctor for being who he was and still is?

Introduction

Peter Carey

The casting of lots is one of the most ancient and, at the same time, one of the most modern practices of humankind. People have been casting lots of one kind or another from time immemorial to today—the word lottery, for example, comes from the same root as "lot."

Basically, there are several types of lots. One type uses some mechanical means to divide things up, or to make choices, or to decide who does what, or who goes first, or who gets what job.

All sorts of devices can be used: throwing dice, pulling straws, picking colored stones or marbles out of a box, using cards, or the ever-popular tossing of a coin: "Heads, I go first; tails, you go first."

There are other types of lots too, usually associated with superstition or trying to read the future or to discover the will of God.

All the aspects of lots were looked at from every possible angle by Saint Thomas Aquinas many centuries ago in a letter entitled *De Sortibus,* meaning "about the casting of lots." Often referred to as an *opusculum* or "short work," it's actually not that short. In English, it comes out to be just under seven and a half thousand words.

De Sortibus is a letter written in response to a friend, and so I have subtitled my translation *A Letter to a Friend about the Casting of Lots.* The exact date of its composition is uncertain, but most scholars think it was written in 1270 or 1271.

The letter is not well known today. This may be for a couple of reasons. First, the language of the letter is Latin, and relatively few people nowadays are taught Latin. This is actually the first time the letter has been published in English, making it available to a general audience. Second, Aquinas's surviving letters (there are about fifteen of them) are not the major works of the great medieval scholar. As such they tend to be eclipsed by those other, more famous, texts.

However, the perennial interest in lots over the centuries is precisely what makes it worthwhile reading and studying *De Sortibus*, even today.

All of the letters of St. Thomas show us an important aspect of his character. Aquinas was a teacher, a writer, and a member of an active and engaged religious order, the Dominicans.

Even though he had a heavy teaching load, and preached and wrote constantly, Thomas never neglected the demands of intellectual charity. When a friend asked him for help on some difficult question, he found the time to reply. That is surely part of the reason why the church regards him as a saint. He was generous with his time and his talent.

Still, Thomas is studied primarily for his masterful synthesis of all prior western Christian thought, notably in his masterpiece, the *Summa theologiae*, as well as his many other major works.

To place *De Sortibus* in context, it's important to know a bit about Thomas Aquinas's major works, principally the *Summa theologiae*.

It is difficult to find words to express adequately how great a work the *Summa* is. Written in his mature years, it ranks as one of the greatest and most influential works of the Christian intellectual tradition.

The *Summa* serves as both a synthesis and compendium of all of the teachings and traditions of Christianity, and scholars of all denominations—Anglican, Roman Catholic, Protestant, and

Orthodox—still turn to it for its clarity and fairness and its dazzling effort to explain the truth of the Christian faith.

Throughout the *Summa*, Aquinas cites a wide range of sources, including the Hebrew and Christian Scriptures, and intellectuals from the pagan (e.g., Plato, Aristotle, and Cicero), Christian (e.g., Augustine, Anselm, Bede), Jewish (e.g., Maimonides), and Muslim (e.g., Averroes) traditions. So, in our modern sense, Aquinas was truly an "ecumenical" thinker and writer.

Aquinas wrote more than seventy works in all: commentaries on Scripture, sermons, commentaries on Aristotle and on other Greek philosophers, and liturgical works of deep spirituality—and, of course, letters, which were often replies to requests for an expert opinion, as is *De Sortibus*.

Probably no work written by the great Dominican philosopher-theologian Thomas Aquinas has a more charming background than this short text. *De Sortibus* is a personal letter, a letter to a friend called James whom Thomas met while they were both living in Orvieto, a city just north of Rome where Pope Urban IV was residing, because Rome was passing through a period of civil unrest.

At that time, Thomas was rapidly gaining a reputation all across Europe for hard work, orthodoxy, and enormous erudition. He was living and working in Naples when Pope Urban asked the authorities of the Dominican Order to assign Aquinas to the Order's priory in Orvieto. The pope wanted him nearby to carry out various commissions for him.

The Order agreed to Thomas's transfer and he arrived in Orvieto when he was only about thirty-five years old, but he was already an ordained priest and a shining star in the new Order founded by St. Dominic in 1216. He had impressively earned the equivalent of a PhD from the University of Paris, then the intellectual center of Europe.

While Thomas Aquinas was in Orvieto his principal task was the intellectual preparation of the young friars who at the time were flocking to enter the Order. But he also had two important commissions to carry out for the pope: first, a short work that would promote unity with the Eastern Orthodox churches; and second, some liturgical work for the newly established Feast of Corpus Christi.

Aquinas carried out both commissions, as well as others, writing what is probably his most mystical and poetic work, the liturgy for the Feast of Corpus Christi, including a hymn for Vespers, which has been sung in churches and processions for centuries, the *Pange Lingua*:

> Down in adoration falling,
> Lo! the sacred Host we hail,
> Lo! o'er ancient forms departing
> Newer rites of grace prevail
> Faith for all defects supplying,
> Where the feeble senses fail.
> —Translated by Edward Caswall, London, 1849.

It was during this time in Orvieto that Thomas became the close friend of the man to whom he would write *De Sortibus* after he had returned to Paris. That friend was James of Tonengo, chaplain to Pope Urban IV.

Tonengo was a small village near Vercelli in northern Italy, in the Piedmont province of Asti. James was a diocesan priest and a canon of the cathedral of Vercelli, but at the time working in the papal curia.

Thomas and James must have hit it off right away because the opening words of *De Sortibus* indicate a deep affection for each other: *Postulavit a me vostra dilectio*. The Latin word *dilectio* is the key. It is a word used to indicate the good will, affection, and esteem that characterizes a true friendship.

After a few years, both Thomas and James left Orvieto to pursue their separate careers. The Order sent Thomas back to Paris, where he would resume his full professorship and accomplish his greatest work, while James returned to Vercelli and his old job as canon of the cathedral.

When the office of bishop of Vercelli became vacant, James ran for bishop, but the electors could not agree on who was to get the job. James was one of the finalists, but no single candidate obtained the majority. They were deadlocked.

The problem was compounded because normally such issues would be settled by the pope, but there was no pope. Clement IV, the successor to Pope Urban IV, had died and the next conclave, held in Viterbo, near Rome—the one that ultimately chose Gregory X—was also deadlocked, and badly so. The standoff lasted almost three years, the longest interregnum in the history of the papacy.

Meanwhile, the electors in Vercelli had no way to break their deadlock. Finally, they agreed to choose their new bishop by lot. At this point Thomas Aquinas enters the scene.

Evidently some of the electors, including perhaps James, had their doubts as to whether a bishop chosen by lot could be regarded as legitimate.

The electors did agree to obtain an expert opinion from Thomas Aquinas, so James wrote to his old friend from Orvieto to settle the matter. Now a famous and highly esteemed professor in Paris, Thomas presented perfect credentials to address the matter.

We do not know, because we do not possess James's letter to Thomas, whether he was in favor of his having obtained the bishopric by lot, or opposed, but a safe guess is that he was hoping for a positive response from Thomas.

Aquinas wrote the letter during the summer break in the academic year. What is most interesting and most generous about the letter is that not only did he take the time from his busy schedule to reply to his friend's request, but also he did so in such a comprehensive way. He sent his friend a veritable treatise on the subject. Aquinas looked at the subject from virtually every possible angle: the purpose of lots, their effectiveness, and, above all, whether the Christian religion should allow them.

We know Thomas thought the whole question of lots was an important one because he later took up the subject again, although much more briefly, in his *Summa theologiae* (Ia–IIae, Q95, art 1–8).

In *De Sortibus*, he also examines many of the places in the Bible where we read about lots. He examines what the early church writers had to say on the subject as well.

Aquinas asks: When can we use lots? How many types of lots are there? Do they ever reveal God's will to us? What about examining entrails or looking at how sticks fall? Is the devil ever involved in lot casting? What about the stars—don't they influence the casting of lots? Not surprisingly, an important issue for Thomas is always the morality of casting lots.

In this letter, Thomas Aquinas looks at the subject of casting lots comprehensively, peeling away systematically layer after layer, all of the different possibilities related to this perennially interesting subject. He touches on free will, on the usefulness of lots, on their efficacy, on their dangers, and on whether God ever speaks to us through the use of lots. Above all, Aquinas reminds us of the importance of the Holy Spirit in the life of the church.

After looking at the question of lots from every conceivable angle, Thomas finally gives James his answer, and what he says may surprise you.

The final words of this wonderful letter from Thomas to his friend James present us with a model of modesty and restraint. Aquinas ends his letter with eight simple words in Latin, *In tantum igitur nunc de sortibus dictum sit*. In English, "And that is all that needs to be said about lots."

I hope you enjoy this entertaining journey into the mind of a great thinker.

PART I

The Translation

De Sortibus
A Letter to a Friend about the Casting of Lots

The translator, Peter Carey, hat in hand in a gesture of respect, studying a small (39 x 14 cm) wooden panel of Saint Thomas Aquinas by the great fifteenth-century Dominican artist Fra Angelico.

This exquisite painting was created by Angelico sometime between 1438 and 1443, and once formed part of the San Marco altarpiece that stood behind the main altar of the Dominican priory of that name in Florence. The altarpiece was later dismantled and scattered to various collectors and museums throughout the world. The painting was acquired by Count Vittorio Cini, an Italian industrialist and art collector, in 1955 and later given by his daughter to the Cini Gallery located in Palazzo Cini on Venice's Grand Canal.

The photograph is printed here with permission from the photographer Anthony Valentino.

A Letter to a Friend about the Casting of Lots

Your affection for me prompted you to write me and ask that I explain what we ought to think about lots. Since a request from a friend certainly deserves a thoughtful response, I have taken some time during this period of vacation in the academic year to clarify my thoughts on this topic.

With regard to lots, we ought to consider the following: the place held by casting lots among similar activities; the goals of lots; their mode and their power; and whether, in accordance with the teaching of the Christian religion, we are permitted to use them.

Chapter I

In which areas we can search for information by using lots

First, we note that certain things exist from necessity, and have always existed. For instance, for God to exist, for 2 + 3 to equal 5, for the sun to rise, and other similar topics. These have either always existed, or always come about in the very same way. In these matters, there is no place for the casting of lots. Indeed, we might even scoff at a person for proposing that we are able to find out anything at all about God's existence or the results of calculation with numbers or the movements of the sun or stars by using lots.

There are other events in nature, such as for the summer to be dry and the winter to be rainy, that take place naturally. Mostly, these events happen in the same way; sometimes, however, they don't, although this may be rare. Yet, contrary or unexpected results do happen occasionally (although less frequently) because some other cause or event may impede or change nature's usual course.

In neither of these cases is there a place for the use of lots. However, if the matters in the second example may affect human life to some degree, we may inquire by lot. For instance, we might use lots to know if a river might overflow and flood homes and fields, or if rain might be plentiful during the summer. But no one should go to the trouble to inquire by lot whether rain will cause a river to overflow in a desert since it's an unlikely event and it also would not affect human life.

Clearly, lots occupy a proper place in human affairs. But because each of us should be careful about those things that concern us personally and those things we share with others in some way, it follows that an inquiry by lots should not be extended to all human affairs. For no person living in France, let us say, would bother to ask about a matter that pertains to the affairs of a person in India, whose life he or she in no way shares. But we might seek information coming from lots about things that in some way pertain to us, or to those people with whom we are connected.

On the other hand, we don't seek information from lots in all of these matters. As we said, we don't seek information coming from lots about something that you could either know through your own effort, or whose effect you can produce. It would be ridiculous, for example, if you inquired by lot whether you should eat a meal, or harvest the crops from the field, or determine whether the shape you see ahead of you is a man or a horse.

We can conclude, therefore, that we look for information coming from lots about areas of human affairs, those that in some way have to do with us and that through our own efforts we can't know the answer to or bring about.

Chapter II

The end to which lots are ordered

B ecause, among the things that have to do with ordinary life, we can see that in certain situations we need an answer by means of lots, it's necessary that the search for information by lots brings this about so that certain things can be adjusted to the service of human life.

Regarding some potential possessions that humans use, first we ought to be intent upon having them; second, upon using them once we have them; and third, knowing the future results of their use.

Because we can't use things that are of service to our life unless we possess them in some way, we need a procedure or process that will help us divide these possessions in a way that we can use them separately—and that leads people to the discernment of lots.

However, when we can divide common things by means of human endeavor and harmony of wills, then lots are not needed. But when common sense doesn't suffice to make this division harmoniously, then we can make the division by lot. According to the Book of Proverbs (18:18), "The lot puts an end to disputes."

Just as there is a distinction of possessions, so also there is one of honors or dignities. For instance, whenever it happens that some are unwilling harmoniously to choose one to receive a dignity or honor, those involved may decide to require that the choice be made by lot.

We see a precedent for this in the Old Law as well, with examples of certain individuals obtaining the office of high priest by lot. We can see it, too, in the Gospel according to Luke (1:9), in which Zechariah was chosen by lot to burn the incense. And, too, Saul was elected king by lot, as we read in 1 Samuel (10:20).

On the other hand, just as a doubt concerning the distribution of honors can happen, we also sometimes experience doubt in the distribution of punishments. Furthermore, if it is believed that someone ought to be punished, but it is not clear who specifically should be punished, some think that this information should be sought by the casting of lots.

For example, to support this, we read in the Book of Jonah (1:7) that Jonah, through the casting of lots, was thrown into the sea. Also, the Book of Joshua (7:14–18) describes that Achan, who stole from a forbidden place, was punished by means of lots.

To summarize, the use of lots is one way in which it can be determined who ought to have either a possession, or a dignity, or a punishment, and we can call this the *distributive lot*, because it helps us determine how something ought to be distributed when we cannot decide how it should be divided. Plus, the word *sortior* (to draw lots) seems to have been taken from *sortes* (lots).

Moreover, we may have doubts about who should have something, or whether we should make use of something, and whether it might be really expedient to do something. For every action is producing something, something useful for itself or for some other reason. Therefore, whenever there are doubts about what we ought to do, if we can resolve these doubts through human prudence, I believe we should have recourse to human counsel.

However, as we see in the Book of Wisdom (9:14), "For the reasoning of mortals is worthless." Where human counsel can't fully respond to uncertainty, human counsel may have recourse to decide the matter by lot.

We read an example of this in the Book of Esther (3:7), where it says, "They cast the lot that they [the Jews] should be destroyed."

Because a lot of this type replaces consultation, we can call it the *advisory lot*, used as it were to seek counsel.

Human beings are frequently concerned about future events, because if we can know the future, we can undertake certain enterprises or avoid certain outcomes. Yet the knowledge of future events exceeds human effort, according to the Book of Ecclesiastes (8:7), "No man has power to retain the spirit, over the day of death."

That is why people sometimes think they ought to use lots to know something about future events, and this can be called the *divining lot,* because people call those people *divines* who foretell certain things about the future. They attribute to themselves what belongs to God, according to the Book of Isaiah (41:23), "Tell us what is to come hereafter, that we may know that you are gods."

Chapter III

The different ways we use lots

We know some people look for knowledge of things that are beyond human effort in various ways. The first way we'll consider is where one asks for clear answers either from God or from demons.

Of this group, those who look to God for answers are the prophets. Those individuals are joined to God by a kind of privileged familiarity. Moreover, they merit to be taught by God about future events or about certain other supernatural things. According to the Book of Amos (3:7), "Surely the Lord God does nothing, without revealing his secret to his servants the prophets." He gives his revelation sometimes to those who are awake through a clear vision, or sometimes, through a dream. According to the Book of Numbers (12:6), "If there is a prophet among you, I the Lord make myself known to him in a vision. I speak with him in a dream."

Many prophets with this particular grace have been warned in sleep about things that have to do with their welfare. That is why the Book of Job (33:18) says, "In a dream, in a vision of the night, when deep sleep falls upon men, while they slumber on their beds, then he opens the ears of men, and terrifies them with warnings, that he may turn man aside from his deed and cut off pride from man; he keeps back his soul from the Pit, his life from perishing by the sword."

In addition to the prophets, there are the diviners. They seek replies from demons; they use certain incantations and sacrifices, or they talk to them, or they receive signs, either while awake or during sleep.

Sometimes human beings seek information about hidden events by receiving signs about what they are seeking to know in other events. There are different kinds of this looking for signs.

For example, some may look at heavenly motions, and may observe movements and positions of stars and planets, and from these observations, they may think they have knowledge of future and hidden things.

Some may be mathematicians or astrologers, who are also called *geneatics* because they interpret things from the implications of the days on which people are born.

Others think that we can learn occult things by observing the movements and sounds of certain animals, and even from a person's sneezing. All these are called *augurs* or *haruspices,* augurs who observe birds, and pay attention to their songs and chattering.

There are yet others who seek knowledge of concealed things from the talk or actions of someone in special situations. This kind of activity is formally called an omen.

Valerius Maximus provides us with an example of this. He tells us that when the consul Lucius Paulus had been about to make war with the Persian king, he returned from court and found his daughter sad. He asked why she was so sad, and she replied, "Persa is dead," because a young puppy named Persa had died. Paulus saw this as an omen foretelling his brilliant triumph over the Persian king.

In addition, some seek to learn hidden things by observing certain figures or patterns that may appear on human bodies, for example, palm reading, which is called *chiromancy.* Or, others study the shoulder blade of a certain animal, and this is called *spatulamancy.*

Some look for hidden knowledge through a third way by creating and conducting a test or experiment and then evaluating the results. This also happens in numerous ways.

In this group is *geomancy* (divination by means of lines and figures or by geographic features), where people might mark off certain small points and then arrange them in various ways. As a result of this process, they believe they can acquire knowledge of certain hidden things.

Other ways to accomplish knowledge of the unknown include concealing some sheets of paper in a hidden place. Certain things are written on some pieces of paper, and on other pieces nothing is written. These determine what ought to happen to people based on which piece of paper they pick, or what benefit or punishment they should receive. Similarly, one might hide straws of different lengths, and thus the way goods are divided among several persons would be allotted by their drawing of longer or shorter straws.

Here, throwing dice is a way to decide how something should be divided, or what ought to be done, or to decide something hidden or yet to come in the future.

A duel would be another way to resolve an issue, except for the fact that one participant overcomes the other primarily through art or strength. Also, judgments by applying a red-hot iron or by being submerged in water or other things of this sort could decide a question, except for the fact that these situations can seriously damage the participants. They seem to require a more express divine authorization than the other means mentioned before.

The word "lot" seems to fit this third kind. Something is done and then when its outcome is examined, something previously hidden is revealed. So, when lots are cast, or thrown into the lap, or some other human action involves lots, the Book of Proverbs (16:33) says, "The lot is cast into the lap."

It is clear from what we have said so far that the lot is a search for knowledge that lies beyond the knowledge that we can obtain by normal human effort. Rather, the lot is an act that we do when dealing with human concerns that pertain directly to us, such as things we own, or use, or want to know. This third category of inquiry about lots can be mixed in with one of the previously mentioned types of inquiry.

This happens with prophetic consultation: for example, when Gideon spread a fleece on the ground, and asked a sign of dew from the Lord, as we read in the Book of Judges (6:37). Or sometimes it is mixed with a consideration of *necromancy*, as in an inspection of sacrificed victims, which involves seeking omens or signs from the viscera of animals sacrificed to demons.

Sometimes, forms of lots might be mixed in with the considerations of astrology, or with observation of *auguries*, as, for example, if the observations of a star or of a particular kind of bird should occur to someone involved in another form of consulting lots. And sometimes divination occurs by observing words spoken for one reason and applying them to a different situation. Or, there is divination by lots when one opens a book and notes the words seen at first glance. And similarly, other different types of lots can be easily collected under mixtures of this third type of inquiry with the other two.

Therefore, the above information delineates the way in which one looks for information by lots.

Chapter IV

The power of lots

We also need to think about whether this search for information by lots is effective. To do this, we need to consider various opinions about how human affairs actually happen. Some think human affairs are regulated by no higher control, but by reason alone, so that whatever occurs in human affairs is completely fortuitous, or the result of accident or chance rather than design. Therefore, according to this opinion, we can't know about future events before they occur, for things that happen by chance are unknowable.

Given this, for people with this opinion, the *divining lot* is a complete waste of time. Similarly, the *advisory lot* is useless, too, because if future happenings are unknowable, consultation by means of such lots would be pointless. Nevertheless, according to those of this opinion, the *distributive lot* can have a place, not as a means of dividing things properly, but so that what can't be determined by reason may at least be left to chance.

However, this opinion limits divine providence, which is infinite. For while those who hold this opinion remove from divine providence those human affairs where clear indications of divine rule are often apparent, they also do an injustice to those human affairs that they see as in flux, without any governance. This process undermines divine worship from every religion, and removes the fear of God from people. Therefore, it should be rejected.

Others have said that all human actions, and their outcomes, and all human affairs, are determined by the stars. Because there's a certain order behind the movement of heavenly bodies, some believe that by considering the movements of the stars, we can accurately determine future human occurrences (unless in cases where they lack experience of it).

Because, according to this opinion, all human actions employed in casting these lots are by necessity from the stars, it follows that even those human actions required for lots are orchestrated by the arrangement of the stars, so that this or that result occurs. For example, if a *geomancer* marks out points in the dirt, people who believe in this claim that his hand is moved according to the power of the heavens in such a way that they proceed from the power of the heavenly disposition.

They say the same thing in other similar situations. For example, they say the future can be revealed from similar actions to the extent that they rule by the power of the heavenly bodies.

Therefore, according to this opinion, the *divining lot* has a place in determining future occurrences. And consequently, so does the *advisory lot*, which depends on a consideration of future events. The *distributive lot* also has a place, not only to this extent, that the distribution of things is left to the judgment of the lot, but also that, as the disposition of the heavens requires, things are considered true.

Because they hold that not only human acts, but also the movements of animals, and of all natural bodies, are subject to the stars, those who think this also say that future events can be known through auguries, and other similar means of inquiry, since they believe these movements or dispositions proceed from the power of the stars. They call stars of this type secondary, because there appears in these only a certain hint of the heavenly bodies.

Just as a sleeping person doesn't have perfect use of reason, but is moved by imagination, there are those who say that dreams have a divining power. The movements of the phantasms, the images that occur in dreams occur with the influence of the heavenly bodies.

For it is not possible that the heavenly bodies make an impression on anything *incorporeal*, because any *incorporeal* thing is more powerful and more transcendent than any body. The human intellect, however, is neither a body nor the power of a bodily organ, as Aristotle showed; otherwise, the human mind would not be able to know the natures of all bodies, just as we wouldn't be able to see all colors if our pupils were tinged by some color.

For that reason, it is impossible for a heavenly body to make an impression on the human intellect. The will is included in the intellect as it is, and it is influenced by the good that is understood through the intellect. Therefore, for the same reason, heavenly bodies are not able to make an impression on it.

All our human acts proceed principally from the intellect and the will. By an investigation of the heavenly bodies, therefore, we cannot predict future human acts for certain through the study of heavenly bodies; and even less by the study of other realities that are influenced by them, like the sounds of birds, or the descriptions of aligned points, and other approaches previously mentioned. It is clear, however, that most of the occurrences in human affairs depend upon human acts. For this reason, we cannot know ahead of time the occurrences in human affairs in the ways just mentioned.

Still, insofar as the outcome of human events depends upon some corporeal causes—for instance, the abundance of crops comes from the dryness of the atmosphere or from rainfall—nothing prevents these from being known ahead of time from an investigation of the stars, and consequently from a consideration of other bodies that follow upon the disposition of the stars. As Augustine says in the fifth book of the *City of God*, "It is not altogether absurd to say that certain fixed stars can influence or can have some power to cause differences in bodies alone—for instance, we see that the seasons of the year come round by the approaching and receding of the sun."

We see also the times of the year change, and by the waxings and wanings of the moon, certain kinds of things are increased or diminished. This is why sailors can foretell oncoming winds and storms by considering the stars and by observing the reactions of animals.

However, we can't reason in a similar way about lots, because we not only investigate human acts through lots, but also the very inquiry itself proceeds through human acts. For that reason, we can't say that the casting of lots itself follows necessarily the arrangement of the heavenly bodies.

In human acts, not only are the intellect and will involved, which are not subject to the influence of the stars, but also the emotional part of the soul is involved, and because it uses a bodily organ, it is necessarily subject to the heavenly bodies. For this reason, one can say that the disposition of the heavenly bodies does provide some inclination in us to do this or that. We might say we are led to this through the apprehension of the imagination, and through the passions or the emotions—namely, anger, fear, and other similar emotions. People are more or less disposed to these emotions according to their bodily make-up, something subject to the disposition of the stars.

Nevertheless, the human person through the intellect and our will can curb the fantasies of the imagination and the passions of the emotions; thus, no necessity from the influence of the stars impels us to act, but only an inclination, which many wisely restrain by moderation.

For this reason, Ptolemy in the *Centiloquium* says, "The wise person rules the stars," that is, controls the inclination that remains from the disposition of the stars.

Foolish people, on the other hand, are led entirely according to these inclinations, as if they are not able to reason. In this they differ little from beasts. According to the Book of Psalms (49:20), "Man cannot abide in his pomp, he is like the beasts that perish." And as Solomon says (Ecclesiastes 1:15), "The number of fools is infinite," meaning that reason rules perfectly only in a few. In many human minds the inclinations of the heavenly bodies forecast what will happen.

This is why astrologers sometimes foretell true things from an examination of the stars, especially about common occurrences, although in particular occurrences, they frequently fail, because reason isn't subject to the heavenly bodies.

Consequently, when people draw points in *geomancy*, they think that this should be done without premeditation, and the one who interprets does so by an inner attraction and not from a deliberation of reason. This is urged for all such consultations.

Although from the above considerations heavenly bodies do not impose some absolute necessity on human acts, but rather may incline some people to act in a certain way, this inclination can't extend to all human happenings. For the heavenly bodies act according to nature. Moreover, it's proper that nature tends toward one thing, just as the action of a natural thing also proceeds from one principle, namely, from the proper form of the thing, which is the principle of natural action.

The intellect, however, acts through forms conceived in the mind, and these forms can be numerous in the same intellect. Consequently, rational powers aren't determined to one thing, but pertain to many. Those things that happen by chance in human events are called accidental—an example would be finding a treasure while digging a grave.

However, what seems to happen *per accidens* actually doesn't. This is because no natural agent can be inclined to events that occur accidentally. A person could have some natural inclination to dig a grave, and, similarly, a person could have a natural inclination to seek a treasure. But that a person finds a treasure while digging a grave does not have a natural cause.

Therefore, an investigation of lots according to the preceding opinion—through a mode of inclination to all human occurrences—can't be successful. But the intellect can understand those things that happen *per accidens* by forming one composite from many things.

Therefore, we know that nothing prevents some things that seem to happen by accident from being preordained by some intellect.

As an example, let us suppose that someone places a stone in the road, and then sends a traveler along that road, and the traveler trips and falls. The traveler's fall is indeed an accident, and it did not happen according to the traveler's intention; it was, however, arranged by the intellect of the person who placed the stone and then sent the traveler on that route.

Accordingly, there are those who say that some events in human affairs that we believe to be fortuitous are, in fact, ordained by some superior intellect. But the supreme intellect is God, who, as divine wisdom causes all things to exist, so that wisdom conserves and moves the same, directing all to their appointed end according to the Book of Wisdom (8:1), "She reaches mightily from one end of the earth to the other, and she orders all things well."

However, divine disposition not only moves bodies, but it also moves human intellects with respect to their proper actions. For the intellect is enlightened by God to know the truth. This is the reason the Psalmist (13:3) begs, "Lighten my eyes, lest I sleep the sleep of death."

Divine power moves human wills to desire and to act. According to the Apostle in his letter to the Philippians (2:13), "For God is at work in you, both to will and to work for his good pleasure."

And because both the intellect and will are the proper principles of human acts, it follows that human acts are subject to divine disposition. According to the Book of Isaiah (26:12), "For you have wrought for us all our works."

So, because both human acts and the motions of external things are subject to divine providence, those events that are bound to happen to each of us proceed from the way God has arranged things, through which things achieve the appointed end of their design. Therefore, the Psalmist (25:5) begs, "Lead me in your truth."

Sometimes we're also led to some good by divine disposition beyond our own intention. This was reflected when the Apostle said in his letter to the Ephesians (3:20), "Now to him who by the power at work within us is able to do far more abundantly than all that we ask or think."

Also, from divine disposition, it turns out that people may fall away from our own intent. According to the Book of Job (5:12),

"He frustrates the devices of the crafty, so that their hands achieve no success."

From time to time, by divine arrangements, some people find themselves in adversities they could not avoid. As the Book of Isaiah (23:7) notes, "Whose feet carried her to settle afar. Who has purposed this against Tyre, the bestower of crowns." After that follows, "The Lord of hosts has purposed it." And then the Book of Jeremiah (10:23) says, "I know, O Lord, that the way of man is not in himself, that it is not in man who walks to direct his steps."

From these examples, therefore, it is clear that human affairs aren't totally subject to human arrangements, but to a divine disposition. Consequently, it happens that when some come to possess more goods than they would be able to use, they are called fortunate. On the other hand, others fall short of those things that they prudently planned and are cast down into disordered evils. They are called unfortunate.

This is not only established on divine authority, but is also proven by the opinions of philosophers. For example, Aristotle, in his book *On Good Fortune*, says, "The starting point of the human person is not reason, but something better. What, then, could be better than knowledge and intellect but God? And for this reason they are rightly called fortunate who, whatever they set out to do, succeed at it without being good at reasoning, for they have in them a principle that is better than intellect and deliberation."

Therefore, according to what has already been determined, an investigation of lots can produce desired results from the divine disposition, both insofar as the occurrences of external things are subject to divine providence and insofar as through divine providence human acts are directed. And that's why it can happen, by God's doing, that our human acts are directed toward such a beneficial effect or course.

For these reasons, the Book of Proverbs (16:33) says, "The lot is cast into the lap, but the decision is wholly from the Lord." And concerning the divine lot that fell upon Matthias, Dionysius says in the *Ecclesiastical Hierarchy*, "Certain others say otherwise, but in my opinion they're not speaking in a religious fashion. I'll give you my opinion. It seems to me that the sacred sayings called the lot *hierarchic*, that is, showing a kind of gift to the hierarchical choir, this is, to the choir of Apostles, namely that 'God had chosen Matthias.'"

Through this, it is clear that it can involve lots when, by a gift of God, there is revealed to us through a certain effect of human acts what the divine disposition is, either in dividing things up, as in the *distributive lot*; or in doing things, as in the *advisory lot*; or in foreknowing future things, as in the *divining lot*.

We ought, moreover, to consider that the divine disposition works by the ministry of certain spirits, according to the Book of Psalms (103:20), "Bless the Lord, O you his angels," and after that there follows, "His ministers of his that do his will!" As a result, the operation of the angels is consistent in all things with the divine disposition, and that's why the judgment is the same about those things done through them as about those things done by the divine disposition.

There are, however, certain deceptive spirits, whom we call demons. Even though these demons reject the divine will to the degree that they can, nevertheless, God uses them for the fulfillment of his will. Similarly, he uses evil human beings to fulfill the purpose of his will, as he used the wickedness of the tyrants to form crowns for the martyrs.

Such corrupt and deceptive spirits try to steal for themselves those things that belong to God so that the people they've duped might show them the honor of divinity. And so it was that the fallen angels involved themselves in the idol-worship that humans made in previous times out of an inordinate regard for the dead, and through the idols they gave answers, so that in this way, too, the demons might procure divine honor for themselves.

Likewise, whether by using lots or in other ways, people stupidly get involved in the occult, demons intrude in an unwelcome way in order to lead them into error under pretext of divination.

Similarly, Augustine says, in the *Literal Interpretation of Genesis*, speaking about mathematicians who foretell future occurrences through the stars, "It should be acknowledged that when truths are spoken by such as these, it comes from a certain hidden instinct which human minds undergo without knowing it. This is the work of the unclean and seducing spirits, since its purpose is to deceive men."

In addition, in the *De Doctrina Christiana*, Augustine says that all types of such divination pertain to pacts made with demons. The opinion of Valerius Maximus does not disagree with this. He says that "human observance rested upon some 'religious' contract, for not upon a chance notion is it believed to depend but upon divine providence."

It is clear from the preceding observations where lots get their power.

Chapter V

Whether it is permitted to use lots

H aving reviewed the pertinent issues so far, it is not hard to see whether it is permitted to use lots. First, it is obvious that no Christian is permitted to make any deals with the devil. For the Apostle in 1 Corinthians (10:20) says, "I do not want you to be partners with demons." This pertains not only to open invocations of the devil, which *necromancers* use, but also to any hidden pacts made with the devil.

Thus Augustine, in his second book on *De Doctrina Christiana*, having observed various human superstitions, adds, "All arts of this sort are either worthless, or are part of harmful superstition, springing out of a dangerous fellowship between human beings and the devil, and ought to be utterly repudiated and avoided by the Christian as the covenants of a false and treacherous friendship."

Also in the Book of Deuteronomy (18:10–20) it says, "There shall not be found among you anyone who burns his son or his daughter as an offering, anyone who practices divination, a soothsayer, or an augur, or a sorcerer, or a charmer, or a medium, or a wizard, or a necromancer."

But it still remains for us to see what inquiries of lots—or of any other divinations where humans enter into pacts with the devil—ought to be branded as superstitious.

We may indeed find the solution to this in the previous words of Augustine if we examine these words carefully. For he states that pacts with demons come about through the arts of worthless or guilty superstitions. An injurious superstition clearly contains something illicit, such as invocations of—and sacrifices to—demons or other similar things.

We call a thing completely useless, on the other hand, when someone uses some particular thing for a purpose that the thing cannot bring about. In fact, it seems to us entirely in vain. Therefore, we call such activities a waste of time.

For example, if a sick person takes medicine for a disease that the medicine can cure, this is not a superstitious vanity. But if someone were to tie some things around the neck that pertain in no way to health, this would seem to be a superstitious empty activity, even according to the opinion of doctors.

Similarly, if mice gnaw into your clothes, will you worry more about some future evil or will you lament the current damage to your clothing? In his second *De Doctrina Christiana,* Augustine sets down many other examples of this type.

To what things the power of lots can extend is also reckoned from what has been said. For we have seen that the power of the heavenly bodies extends itself to corporeal effects, but not to change our free will. Therefore, if someone consults an astrologer as to whether a future summer will be dry or rainy, it is not a useless consultation, as it would be if someone should consult an astrologer about whether in digging a grave one would come upon a treasure, or some answer to another question. For this reason, such a consideration pertains to the involvement of demons, who like to involve themselves in our human superstitions.

We should note the same thing about auguries. If someone predicted future rain from the frequent squawking of a crow, it is not a pointless superstition. Animals are moved by a certain natural instinct from the influence of the heavenly bodies, in accordance with the disposition of the air, to the knowledge of the weather, because it is necessary for their nature. We see this agrees with the Book of Jeremiah (8:7), "Even the stork in the heavens knows her times; and the turtledove, swallow, and crane keep the time of their coming."

Similarly also, if from the sudden flight of birds someone should announce that some danger is hiding in that place where the birds had flown away from, this is not a superstition, but human perspicacity. But if the motions or chattering of birds seem to foretell something about human actions, this is superstition. The same also should be noted with regard to lots and other similar matters. Whatever can have a sure cause, either natural, human, or divine, is not superstitious, but only those things are problems and superstitions that cannot have a sure cause. These pertain to the company of demons, who sometimes make things happen in such a way as to envelop peoples' souls in pointless activity.

In the Book of Psalms (40:4), it says, "Blessed is the man who makes the Lord his trust, who does not turn to the proud to those who go astray after false gods!" The sacred canons, therefore, condemn these lots, which, since they come about from harmful and useless superstition, pertain to the company of the demons.

If, however, those things that have a natural or human cause are permissible, so much the more are those that rest on divine assistance. For it pertains to man's beatitude, according to the same psalm, that the name of the Lord be his hope. Consequently, if through the casting of lots someone seeks divine judgment, this is not in itself a sin. Concerning the psalm, Augustine says, "My lots are in your hands. The lot is no evil thing, but it can be an event, in cases of human doubt, of indicating the Divine Will."

It should be known, however, that sin can happen in four ways in lots of this type. First, if someone should think that there should be recourse to lots without any necessity, for this seems to test God. For example, if someone knows what he should do, omitting to do it draws out divine judgment. For it says in 2 Chronicles (20:12), "We do not know not what to do, but our eyes are upon you."

Second, if divine judgment is sought through lots without due reverence and devotion, even in necessity. Bede, in his *Commentary on the Acts of the Apostles*, says, "If compelled by some necessity, they think that God should be consulted after the example of the Apostles, by lots, they should observe this: the Apostles themselves acted after having gathered together the band of the brethren, and having poured forth prayers to God."

Third, if the divine Scriptures are turned toward human and worldly business. This is why Augustine says in his *Reply to the Inquiries of Januarius*: "[Regarding] those who draw lots from the pages of the Gospels, although it could be wished that they would do this rather than run around consulting demons, nevertheless, I do not like this custom of wishing to turn the divine oracles to worldly business and the vanity of this life."

Fourth, if some should perchance wish to leave to lots that which should be done through divine inspiration, as when men should be promoted to ecclesiastical dignities by agreement in an election, this is a decision the Holy Spirit makes. Consequently, in elections of this kind, it is unlawful for the lot to be used. For it would be an injury towards the Holy Spirit, who instructs human consciousness so that it judges correctly; according to 1 Corinthians (2:15), "The spiritual man judges all things."

However, "He who is chosen by lot is not grasped by human judgment," as Ambrose says in his *Commentary on the Book of Luke*. Consequently, Bede, in his *Commentary on the Acts of the Apostles*, also says, "Matthias, ordained before Pentecost, is selected by lot, because the plentitude of the Holy Spirit had not yet poured forth in the church; however, the seven deacons selected afterwards were ordained not by lot, but by the choice of the disciples, the prayer of the Apostles, and the imposition of hands."

The previously described necessity, however, by which it is lawful to implore divine judgment through lots seems especially to have legitimacy with regard to the *advisory lot*, because even among upright ancients we frequently find some to have consulted God in doubtful affairs, as 1 Kings (1 Samuel 30:8) states that "And David inquired of the Lord, 'Shall I pursue after this band? Shall I overtake them?'"

A necessity of this type also may pertain to the *distributive lot*, whenever disagreements among people concerning the distribution of things cannot otherwise be settled except by being committed through lots to divine judgment. According to the Book of Proverbs (18:18), "The lot puts an end to disputes and decides between powerful contenders."

The necessity of the *distributive lot* can occur not only in dividing things, but also in the division of things that are to be done by different people as well. Augustine, in his *Letter to Honoratus*, says, "If among the servants of God, there is a debate as to which of their number should remain, lest by the flight of all the church be left destitute; and who should flee, lest by the death of all the church be left destitute; if this debate is not able to be terminated in some other way, it appears to me that those who are to remain and those who are to flee should be chosen by lot."

In the same way, the need for the lot occurs when something that is to be given to many can only be given to one. Augustine says in *De Doctrina Christiana*, "For suppose that you had a great deal of something, and felt bound to give it away to somebody who had none, and suppose that it could not be given to more than one person. If two persons presented themselves, neither of whom had either a greater need, or a closer relationship, or a greater claim on you than the other, you could do nothing fairer than choose by lot the recipient to whom you would give what could not be given to both."

And because the office of an earthly dignity is ordained to dispense temporal things, we are allowed to have recourse lawfully to lots of this type if the choice cannot be made in a harmonious way. That said, rulers shouldn't be sought by lot, but by finding someone who is prudent and hard working. Yet it is more tolerable to seek a secular ruler by lot than to burden the people with dissensions. Considering someone who is an authority in spiritual matters there is another consideration, which we have already discussed.

In the *divining lot*, this previously mentioned need does not seem to occur. As the Lord spoke to the disciples, "it is not for you to know times or seasons which the Father has fixed by his own authority" (Acts 1:7).

Nevertheless, if it be necessary that the future be determined either for the safety of the church or of some individual person, this will be made known to the faithful through the Holy Spirit, concerning whom the Lord spoke in the Gospel according to John (16:13), "And he will declare to you the things that are to come." It is lawful to seek divine judgment about future events of this type by means of the *advisory lot*, as we read in the Book of Judges (6:36), where Gideon sought from the Lord whether by his hand the people of Israel would be saved by seeking a sign in the fleece.

Because the *distributive lot* can have a place even when human affairs occur by luck, as has already been said, some use of the distributive lot is permitted—not in order to seek a divine judgment—but by understanding it to be essentially the same as the luck involved in rolling the dice. However, this does not lack the taint of vanity.

And that is all that needs to be said about lots.

PART II

The Essays

The image of Saint Thomas Aquinas is printed here with permission from Monastery Icons.

Biographies of
the Essay Contributors

Rev. Dr. Andrew Davison

Dr. Davison is the Starbridge Senior Lecturer in Theology and Natural Sciences in the Faculty of Divinity of Cambridge University. Before his move into theology he was a scientist, and he holds undergraduate degrees and doctorates in both natural sciences (Merton College, Oxford) and theology (Corpus Christi College, Cambridge). He taught Christian doctrine at Oxford and at Cambridge before his current appointment and was junior chaplain of Merton College, Oxford. In 2015 he was made a canon of St. Albans Cathedral in the UK: the first canon philosopher in the Church of England. He has been a fellow of Corpus Christi College since 2014, and Dean of Chapel since 2019. He is a frequent lecturer and visitor to the United States. The author of more than ten books and numerous articles, Father Davison's most recent book is *Participation in God: A Study in Christian Doctrine and Metaphysics* (2019), a work that draws extensively on the writings of Saint Thomas Aquinas.

Rev. Dr. Matthew Fox

One of the most popular and widely acclaimed spiritual writers and lecturers of our day, Matthew Fox is the author of more than thirty-five books, which have been translated into seventy-five languages. Studying at the Institut Catholique de Paris, he was introduced by Pere Chenu to the creation spirituality tradition and has spent his life trying to share that tradition by creating schools and pedagogy appropriate to teaching spirituality in the twenty-first century. He has written three books on Hildegard of Bingen and on Meister Eckhart. Among his other books are *Original Blessing, The Coming of the Cosmic Christ, A Spirituality Named Compassion,* and a major study on Aquinas that translates numerous works never before translated into English, *Sheer Joy: Conversations with Thomas Aquinas on Creation Spirituality,* and most recently, *The Tao of Thomas Aquinas: Fierce Wisdom for Hard Times.* A Dominican in good standing for thirty-four years, he was dismissed under pressure from Cardinal Ratzinger for teaching the Divine Feminine and liberation theology. Welcomed into the Episcopal church, he created the "Cosmic Mass" to reinvent forms of liturgy and has launched with two young leaders the Order of the Sacred Earth.

Dr. Deirdre Good

Dr. Good was born in Kenya and grew up in the United Kingdom. She then came to the United States and first earned her STM in 1976 at Union Theological Seminary and then her ThD at Harvard Divinity School in 1983. Her field of specialization is New Testament Studies. In 1992 she joined the faculty of The General Theological Seminary in New York where she was a professor and academic dean for twenty-eight years and academic dean for two years. Her books include *Jesus' Family Values* (2006) and *Mariam, the Magdalen, and the Mother* (2005). Dr. Good's most recent book is *Courage Beyond Fear: Re-formation in Theological Education,* co-edited with Katie Day (2019). She was Theologian in Residence at Trinity Church Wall Street, and she teaches presently at The Stevenson School for Ministry in the Diocese of Central Pennsylvania. Dr. Good is semi-retired and now lives in Maine.

Rev. Tobias Stanislas Haller BSG

Father Haller, the former rector of Saint James Episcopal Church, Fordham, New York, is now retired and lives in Baltimore. He is a member of the Brotherhood of St. Gregory, a community of friars within the Anglican Communion. He is the author of many articles and books, including his recent *Re+Membering God: Human Hope & Divine Desire* (2019); *Reasonable and Holy: Engaging Same-Sexuality* (2009); *What About Sex? A Little Book of Guidance* (2017), and the best- selling revision of *The Episcopal Handbook* in 2015. He is a regular reviewer for the Anglican Theological Review.

Rev. Boniface Ramsey

Father Ramsey was ordained a Dominican priest in 1973. He obtained a doctorate from the Institut Catholique de Paris and was granted the title of Master of Sacred Theology from the Dominican Order. His writings and translations have been mostly in the area of patristics, including the widely used *Beginning to Read the Fathers* (1985). He is currently the general editor of *The Works of St. Augustine: A Translation for the 21st Century.* After serving for many years as a seminary professor, Father Ramsey turned to pastoral work. In 2004, he joined the Archdiocese of New York and now serves as administrator of the Church of Saint Joseph-Yorkville in Manhattan.

Dr. Christopher Wells

Dr. Wells is executive director and publisher of the Living Church Foundation, overseeing all of its publishing and teaching initiatives, fundraising, and staff. He completed doctoral studies in historical theology at the University of Notre Dame. He earned a BA at St. Olaf College and MAR at Yale Divinity School. He is Affiliate Professor of Theology at the General Theological Seminary and Nashotah House, where he teaches courses on Augustine of Hippo, Thomas Aquinas, and Anglican ecclesiology. He has published articles on Aquinas and ecclesiology in various journals, and since 2011 has served as theological consultant to the Anglican-Roman Catholic Consultation in the US (ARC-USA). He lives in Dallas.

1

Anglican Reverence for Aquinas

Andrew Davison

Aquinas commands the attention and affection of Anglicans like never before. His works feature prominently in courses at theological colleges. Among Catholic-minded Anglican theologians, he serves as a principal inspiration. Even among Protestant-minded Anglican theologians, few fail to hold him in high regard.

Why has his star risen so high? Here, let us briefly explore *why* Aquinas appeals to so many Anglicans, and *how* they put his ideas to work.

In twenty-first century theology, few trends can compete with the idea of *retrieval*: the conviction that theology is most lively, and most able to speak to our own age, when we source it from the best of the past theological traditions offered.

Anglicanism has always been a tradition of retrieval. The Reformation saw a theological return to Scripture and the writers of the early church. Think of Archbishop Matthew Parker raking through his great haul of manuscripts, many going back to Anglo-Saxon times, looking for models of church order independent of Rome.

Slightly later, Caroline divines such as Lancelot Andrewes produced magnificent sermons and works of devotion, again by drawing on patristic traditions. In subsequent centuries, the evangelical revival sought a return to Scripture, as did the Oxford Movement, alongside a further flowering of patristic scholarship and translation. Aquinas belongs in Anglican theology today as a figure of retrieval. As someone to retrieve from, he features as prominently as Augustine or Calvin, but there is more to it than that. Aquinas set an important example as a great retriever himself. It is no coincidence that the standing of Aquinas among Anglicans has risen in step with reappraisal of his projects and sources.

Scripture has always held pride of place for Anglicans, and the scholarly community now recognizes Aquinas as a biblical scholar of distinction. Indeed, commentaries on Scripture form the largest part of his writings. Anglicanism has always also been invested in the writings of the early church, and few figures in Christian history have been more attentive to those writings than Aquinas.

His works are shot through with quotations from the church fathers, both Western and Eastern. Aquinas's discussion of the casting of lots (*De Sortibus*), translated in this volume, provides ample evidence of his reverence and knowledge of both Scripture and patristic writers.

Other overlaps come to mind. Many Anglican theologians today have a foot in both doctrine and philosophical theology. So did Aquinas. No small part of his greatness rests on his mastery of both Aristotle and, to a lesser degree, Platonism.

On top of that, Anglicans also now notice more than ever that they stand shoulder to shoulder with members of other religious traditions. We find Aquinas drawing respectfully upon both Jewish and Islamic writings, and we might see his debt to pagan religious Platonism as a third example of inter-religious dialogue.

Talk of Anglicanism as a "middle way" between Catholicism and Protestantism can be vague and unhelpful, but there *is* something to it. There have been swings and extremes, and it is possible to be a loyal Anglican and still lie away from a mean. Nonetheless, since the Reformation, and firmly since the restoration of the church and its liturgy in 1662, Anglicanism has held together elements both Catholic and Protestant, each tempering the other: with a liturgy containing many medieval elements, but in English, with the Bible as foundation; and with the fathers as the reliable guides for how to read it; with a monarch, in the UK, who could not be a Roman Catholic, but who was anointed and crowned by church leaders who had to be bishops.

I have mentioned the standing of Aquinas among both Catholics and Protestants today. Not everyone will follow him on every point—not, necessarily on transubstantiation or purgatory—but on the doctrines of the creeds, he is widely celebrated as an expert exponent of common Christianity. Within a broad church, like Anglicanism, Aquinas can be, and often is, a unifying figure.

So, if the standing of Aquinas among Anglicans has never been stronger, it really is Thomas himself who holds their attention, not later systems or traditions built upon his works (Thomism).

A second defining characteristic of an Anglican use of Aquinas is to treat him as a beginning rather than an end. The English priest Eric Mascall put this well (Mascall being as committed and accomplished a scholar of Aquinas as the Anglican Communion has ever produced). In *He Who Is*, his first great work of metaphysics, he wrote about why he would not follow Aquinas in a "restrictive and reactionary" way:

> I do not consider *Thomas locutus, causa finita*: "Thomas has spoken, the case is closed" as the last judgment to be passed on any theological problem; though my approach might be summed up in the words, *Thomas locutus, causa incepta*: "Thomas has spoken, the matter is begun."

Mascall recognized that his own thoughts would not always agree with Aquinas, but added, "I do not think that in any case it matters very much; Saint Thomas certainly will not mind."

"Thomas has spoken, the matter is begun" shows a profound love for what Aquinas thought, valued even more for the sake of what he can help us to think through in our own time.

As an example of that approach, rather than *Thomas has spoken, the case is closed*, one can survey the phalanx of Anglican theologians today for whom Aquinas is a central inspiration, even their primary inspiration, and note that—almost to a man or woman—most of these Anglican thinkers celebrate the ordination of women with enthusiasm, and many feel the same about same-sex relationships: not in spite of the theological tradition, represented prominently by Aquinas, but *because* of it.

Of course, Anglicans do not have a corner on the market with that approach to Aquinas: *Thomas has spoken, the matter is begun.* Plenty of our Roman Catholic colleagues would say precisely the same.

But then, what could be more characteristically Anglican than *not* to claim to have cornered the market? As many have put it, the characteristic Anglican claim is not to superiority or even to distinctiveness, but simply to be one valid part of the whole—of the catholic church and tradition—showing good instincts and being glad that they are also found elsewhere.

Now, we need to think about *how* Aquinas features among Anglican writers: first, in *his own writings*, rather than through any necessarily deep familiarity with Thomism (traditions and systems elaborated from his works), and second, with Aquinas as *a place to start*, rather than a place that holds all the answers.

And finally, I would like to say something about why the tenor of Aquinas's thought has so appealed to Anglicans.

There is a profound overlap of outlook between Anglicanism and Thomas over how God's gifts in creation relate to the transforming and elevating work of grace. In the best sense, there is something earthy and celebratory about both traditions, seeking not to escape from human nature or society, but rather that God should make them whole.

In Aquinas, we see that in his conviction that nature remains good, despite its fallenness: that there is a glorious, variegated goodness of creation, which comes from God and manifests God's own goodness. Redemption and grace elevate, strengthen, and perfect that nature; they do not extinguish it and start again.

We see it in the sense that Christian virtue, even at its most extraordinary, builds on strengths that are natural to every human being; or that what is naturally most dear to us, as Thomas notes, such as our own lives, and those of our families, can also be most worthy of our duty and care.

When it comes to that outlook in Anglicanism, consider its love and nurture for learning, music, craft, and architecture; consider its pursuit of a gentle reasonableness; consider its account of marriage as hallowing something already marked by a grace given in nature, as "a gift of God in creation and a means of his grace, a holy mystery." Think of George Herbert's ideal, *The Country Parson*, whose "cure of souls" leads seamlessly to concern for health of body and human community.

Think also of the Anglican departure from its Reformation kin in political matters: away from the "two kingdoms" view of political power in Lutheranism, where the state has a divine authority distinct from the church, and from Calvinist theocracy, upholding instead (in its English cradle) a sacral monarchy, where church and state are neither merged nor set apart.

Considered this way, we arrive at the heart of why the noble and dignified practices and instincts of Anglicanism fit so beautifully alongside the intellectual glories of Aquinas, and his legacy.

Anglicanism and Aquinas concur around a generous Christian humanism. We see that concurrence in vivid display in the charming letter, *De Sortibus: A Letter to a Friend about the Casting of Lots.*

2

Use of Scripture in *De Sortibus*

DEIRDRE GOOD

Reading Scripture through the eyes of Thomas Aquinas expos-
es today's readers to medieval exegesis, combining the dia-
lectical requirement of precision with alertness to a metaphorical
transmission of the message. Aquinas interprets Scripture using a
literal sense while simultaneously alerting readers to deep spiritual
senses: allegorical, moral, and anagogical.

The literal sense of Scripture indicates an investigation of
what God seeks to communicate. Going beyond the surface of the
texts, it leads to deeper meaning. For example, a reader's attention
is drawn to certain figures of speech; when speaking of the soul we
are to understand the soul representing an entire human being.
Aquinas describes the first method of speaking as humble since it
is the means of conveying wisdom; the second one, embellishment,
is used to convince others in a discussion or dispute; the third one
is an element of beauty inviting enjoyment of the listener.

These three methods allude to the classical practice of rheto-
ric and interpretation: to teach; to move or persuade; and to please
or delight, from Cicero, *Orator* (21.69) and quoted by Saint Augustine in his work *On Christian Doctrine*.

In regard to instances of using lots in Scripture, the letter *De Sortibus* starts with the literal, categorizing use of lots as first distributive, meaning when voluntary distribution is impracticable or divisive; for example, as Proverbs (18:18) explains, "Casting the lot settles disputes among powerful opponents." It then covers advisory, meaning decisions about courses of action as, for example, Proverbs (16:33) indicates, "Lots are cast into the lap, but the outcome is determined by the Lord." The last type moves beyond the literal, divining to know the future. The last case is qualified; there must be a real need accompanied by reverence and devotion, and recourse to lots cannot replace divine inspiration manifested by the Holy Spirit.

The medieval scholar Thomas Aquinas wrote *De Sortibus* on the permissibility of casting lots in an episcopal election, in response to a request from James of Tonengo, a chaplain of Pope Urban IV regarding his own episcopal election. The answer from Aquinas is straightforward: using lots to determine the outcome of an episcopal election is not permitted. Aquinas continues: in cases of an election for ecclesiastical office, the Holy Spirit creates electoral unanimity; to cast lots in such cases would be a sin against the Holy Spirit.

To buttress his argument, Aquinas cites three scriptural passages.

First, 1 Corinthians (2:15), "A spiritual person judges all things."

Second, Aquinas cites Ambrose in his *Commentary on Luke* (1:9), describing the office of Zechariah as elected high priest to go annually into the second tabernacle to offer himself for the sins of the people at a time when the true high priest was as yet unknown, ". . . for he who is chosen by lot is not grasped by human judgment."

Third, following the argument of Ambrose, Aquinas cites Bede in his *Commentary on the Acts of the Apostles*, who says, "Mathias ordained before Pentecost, is selected by lot, because the plenitude of the Holy Spirit had not yet poured forth in the church; however, the seven deacons selected afterwards were ordained not by lot, but by the choice of the disciples, the prayer of the Apostles, and the imposition of hands."

In the entire text, this is the only place three readings of Scripture made or cited in agreement by Aquinas from revered patristic authors are combined to bear on the one key argument: election for office in Christian community must be effectuated not by lots but by the Holy Spirit.

It is worth noting that the *Catena Aurea* (*Golden Chain*), a compilation of patristic commentaries on the four Gospels, was compiled by Saint Thomas in Orvieto during the same period when he wrote the *De Sortibus*.

The readings of Ambrose and Bede on Luke (1:9) occur also in the volume of Luke in the *Catena Aurea*. The *Catena Aurea* was translated by a team and published by John Henry Newman in 1841, while Newman was still an Anglican and working with Edward Pusey on a series translating and making accessible essential patristic texts in English.

3

Four Gifts for Our Time

Matthew Fox

Reading this letter, I was especially struck by four contributions Thomas makes to our world today. One is his ecumenism; his willingness to discuss things that many of today's religious pooh-bahs would not even touch: astrology, palm reading, and—the very theme of the letter—the casting of lots! Thomas, while bringing his considerable intellectual gifts to the table, does not dismiss these practices out of hand even as he navigates his way adroitly through biblical examples of dealing with fate and lot casting. He concludes, however, that they are not fitting for the particular ecclesial decision making that is the focus of the question he addresses in this letter.

A second theme that leaps out at me is the primary role of the Holy Spirit in his ultimate argument why the casting of lots does not suffice for electing prelates. This is very important for a theology of the Holy Spirit, which so often goes ignored or is undeveloped in Western religion, which much prefers to focus on sin and redemption and the cross of Jesus.

While claiming to be Trinitarian, Western Christianity has often neglected the God of creation and even more so this role of

God the Holy Spirit, which so often gets short shrift. (Might that be because, as Aquinas knew well, the Spirit is feminine in Hebrew, Greek, and the Bible? Or because the Spirit "blows where it will" and is integral to creativity and thus very hard to control?)

But Aquinas puts the Spirit and the great dramatic liturgical texts of Pentecost—so cosmic and so dramatic—at the very climax and crescendo of his letter. Thomas insists the Spirit is alive and well in his day—it is even present at the voting for a new bishop.

By implication, of course, he is declaring how alive and well the Holy Spirit is in our day. We need to be open to its powerful influence by way of the choices we make and the creative work we engage in. Elsewhere Aquinas says, "The same Spirit who hovered over the waters at the beginning of creation hovers over the mind of the artist at work" (I, Q. 66, Art.3). What could be more affirming about human creativity than that observation? That the Spirit that birthed the universe is eager to birth human ideas at work? He recognizes the Holy Spirit as the instructor of all of humankind.

Third, Aquinas identifies this Spirit as the same Spirit that anointed the prophets, including Jesus (and, of course, "Christ," as Thomas asserts often in his work, means "the anointed one"). So this letter hints strongly at the prophetic role that all Christians are meant to incorporate. This prophetic role comes with our "anointing" at baptism and confirmation. Aquinas recognizes prophets as those who look to God for an answer . . . "from a privileged familiarity with God."

We, too, are to be mystics (lovers) and prophets—the "mystic in action," as William Hocking puts it, or one who "interferes" with injustice, as Rabbi Heschel puts it. Thomas recognizes that "dreams and visions" often inform the prophetic awareness.

The summary of the Christian life, the imitation of Christ, is found in those two words, *mystic* and *prophet*, the former is our Yes to life; the latter is our No that is spoken when we stand up against injustice.

The fourth contribution I appreciate in this letter from Friar Thomas is how it culminates in *his theology and spirituality of work*. Aquinas, like his brilliant disciple Meister Eckhart, has profound and much needed wisdom to offer about work as a spiritual practice. Indeed, when I wrote *The Reinvention of Work* twenty-six years ago, I found myself returning time and time again to Aquinas's and Eckhart's teachings about work because their contributions are so substantive and rich.

In this letter, Aquinas is setting the ground for a theology of work by invoking first, the importance of ecumenism, second, the role of Spirit, and third, the demands of prophecy. All these elements constitute a bona fide and substantive contribution to a theology of work.

One can grasp Thomas's love of work not only in theory, but also in practice. His immense output in only twenty years of writing (while teaching and travelling also) speaks volumes—quite literally—of his devotion to his work.

In his writings and also in his life itself, he practiced what he preached. For example, in agreeing to write this letter, *De Sortibus*, he put aside time during his summer vacation to do so. He offers an extended treatise and demonstrates his generosity by expanding James's question, giving him far more than he asked for in order to show him the full range of the various aspects related to lots. As Pasquale Porro says in *Thomas Aquinas: A Historical and Philosophical Profile*, Aquinas wrote "a veritable treatise, however small, on everything related to lots" (p. 359).

One can see from these teachings, and from the example of his own life, how important work was to Aquinas—how indeed for him it was one's prayer. It is significant how true students of Aquinas, such as Meister Eckhart and my mentor, Pere M. D. Chenu, wrote deeply about work, including how work can be a spiritual practice.

Work is our gift to God and our neighbors, living and generations from today. It is creative; the Holy Spirit moves over the mind of the worker at work. (In the particular case addressed in this letter, the voting of the canons for a new bishop.) Our work is our art and in Otto Rank's words, "The artist is one who wants to leave behind a gift." Our work is the gift we want to leave behind. Like

Aquinas did; not only in this modest but crystal-clear letter, but in all of his writings, his vast and deep volume of works.

Thank you, Brother Thomas! Thank you to Peter Carey for bringing this letter alive to us today. And thank you to all who welcome the Spirit of Art and Creativity into our common work, the great work, of compassion and justice-making in a time of challenge to the earth and to humanity that we face together.

4

Divination and Deliberation

Tobias Haller

We need to reflect on a similarity between the charismatic authority of the apostles and the authority of rabbinic councils when making decisions for the good of the people. Making deliberative decisions on questions of faith and order form much of the substance of rabbinic thought and procedure. Convergence emerges in answer to the question, what is the cause of this decision-making? The answer, for rabbis and church fathers alike, is ultimately God. The convergence for the bestowal of this gift and charge is Pentecost: in rabbinic tradition, the feast commemorates the giving of the Torah on Mount Sinai; in Christian tradition, the descent of the Spirit upon the apostles.

The Law and Spirit are here seen as parallel manifestations of the personal power of God, given to humankind for specific ends, and each endures by descent upon and presence with an assembled body of human leaders.

The first verse of the Mishnaic tractate *Aboth* sums up both principles: "Moses received the Law from Sinai and committed it to Joshua, and Joshua to the elders, and the elders to the Prophets; and the Prophets committed it to the men of the Great Synagogue.

They said three things: Be deliberate in judgment, raise up many disciples, and make a fence around the Law."

The rest of this chapter details the further rabbinic *traditio* in much the same way as historians of the early church described the transmission of apostolic tradition. That the earlier rabbis are contemporaries of the early apostles renders the congruence even more striking.

The other important congruence—the call to rely on judgment rather than chance in reaching decisions for the good of the church—is the charge to be "deliberate in judgment," a call echoed in the final verse *Aboth* (1:18): "by three things is the world sustained: by truth, by judgment, and by peace . . . ."

The concept of deliberative justice is central to rabbinic thinking—not just for good order, but as an essential of the human world itself. The ultimate purpose of law is the good of that world; the exercise of jurisprudence, including deliberation and development of interpretations of law, participates in the *tikkun ha-olam*, repairing the world damaged by injustice and wrong.

So central is the need for deliberative judgment that the rabbinic tradition holds the establishment of courts of justice to be among the universal commandments of God for all humankind—not just for the Jewish world, but for all the descendants of Noah, in recognition of their *humane* and rational character.

Justice is to be *deliberate*, not arbitrary. And this would seem to rule out the use of lots where matters of justice are concerned.

However, just as Thomas addressed the objection that lots are permissible because the apostles used them in choosing Matthias, we need to address the obvious fact that lots are employed in Jewish tradition, documented in both the written and oral Torah. Thomas cites a few of the scriptural instances in *De Sortibus*.

The most trivial response to this objection is that the lots from the Law—written and oral—are just that: divinely mandated law, procedures for making specific determinations in specific cases; divination at the direction of the Divine.

To cite two examples from Thomas's survey: the election of Saul as king in 1 Samuel 10:20 is preceded by and confirms his prophetic and charismatic anointing by Samuel in the previous chapter. What amounts to a trial by hazard to determine who violated the covenant by retaining items meant for devotion to destruction (Joshua 7:14–18) is undertaken only in response to a direct verbal instruction from the Lord. Obviously, any form of divination carried out in response to a divine ordinance will have divine authority: there is tacit recognition that God is at work in these lots, and they are not subject to chance.

These especially holy lots are connected with the priesthood and restricted to particularly serious forms of inquiry. They are intimately connected with the priesthood and the temple, and with the ministry of the prophets.

This brings up another dichotomy, related to the change from lots to deliberation in the work of the apostles, as parallel to the use of lots in the biblical and rabbinic tradition: the distinction between a priestly versus a prophetic approach to making determinations.

As we have seen, lots have a priestly, ceremonial character; they almost always involve paraphernalia of some sort, and so there is an aura of *techné* about them. One recalls Arthur C. Clarke's Third Law, that any sufficiently advanced technology is indistinguishable from magic. No doubt, even in, perhaps *especially* in, pagan cultures, the fascination with the *equipment* and *procedure* that accompanies oracular divination adds to the effect on the mind and heart of the one making inquiry.

Prophets, on the contrary, speak for God out of the store of charismatic inspiration, and it is the power of their charisma that promotes their authority. The biblical text illustrates this distinction in one of the examples cited by Thomas: the charismatic anointing of Saul as king is followed by a procedural casting of lots, with great ceremony, to confirm his election.

Thomas alludes to the distinction of a special class of divine divination in chapter IV, citing Dionysius, and concluding that such *thearchic* lots may be involved when, "by a gift of God, there is revealed to us through a certain effect of human acts what the divine disposition is, either in dividing things up, as in the *distributive lot*;

or in doing things, as in the *advisory lot*; or in foreknowing future things, as in the *divining lot*."

Thomas does not suggest that the eleven acted wrongly when they made use of lots; his critique, following Bede, is against those who would use their action as an excuse to do the same in the present day.

A more substantive response to the objection is to note that most of the lots mandated in the Torah and Mishnah are *distributive*. Lots are used to distribute the various tasks of the priesthood among the available priests. The concern shown in the Mishnah is for fairness in the distribution of work, so for example, those who have never had the privilege of preparing the incense are to be given first chance to cast lots.

Safety is also a concern, as when a priestly rush to remove ashes from the altar resulted in a broken leg, lots are then introduced to avoid such incidents.

From Thomas's perspective, distribution is the least problematical use for lots, as they involve the mere division of things among those entitled to or responsible for them.

Where these distributive lots have the support of a divine mandate, there is no question as to their rightful employment.

There is one more important parallel between Thomas's work and rabbinic tradition: the sense in which both the rabbinic council and the apostles owe their authority to make decisions to a divine disposition, a divine condescension.

Just as Thomas's letter cites Pentecost as the crucial point at which God bestows the Holy Spirit, along with the authority to make decisions, on the apostles, so too rabbinic tradition holds that Pentecost—Shavuoth, the Feast of Weeks—is the day on which the Holy One gives the Law to Moses on Sinai. With that *giving* comes responsibility.

That responsibility is worked out and expressed in differing but related ways in the two contexts of church and rabbinic council.

The apostles take responsibility and show confidence in reaching decisions in the name of the Holy Spirit. In the rabbinic tradition, the authority is not attributed to the continued action of the Holy One, but is expressed in terms of even greater responsibility: for authority is held to have been transferred, at Sinai, to Moses and the line of descent stemming from him, and responsibility is expected from those to whom the authority is given.

This transfer of authority explicitly includes the use of lots in the instance cited by Thomas regarding the concealed theft of devoted things in Joshua 7.

The authority of the rabbis to work in a logical and pneumatic fashion—using their deliberative and rational faculties rather than relying on lots—is confirmed in a passage from the Palestinian Talmud, where Moses is urged to "Go according to the majority— if the majority rules someone is acquitted, they are acquitted; if they rule the person is convicted, they are convicted."

The rabbis came to accept the maturity bestowed upon them—the gift of the Law and the rational mind, able to look into that Law and render decisions, rather than resorting to miraculous or magical sources for inspiration.

5

Aquinas and the Fathers
of the Church

Boniface Ramsey

Whoever reads Saint Thomas's brief but nonetheless strikingly characteristic work *De Sortibus* will notice that he makes use of three different kinds of sources, or authorities. One of these is the classic writers of Greek and Roman antiquity, whom Thomas refers to four times—Valerius Maximus, an early first-century compiler and anecdotalist (twice), and the better-known Aristotle and Ptolemy (once each). A second source is Scripture, both the Old and New Testaments, which Thomas refers to about three dozen times. And a third is the fathers of the church, whom he cites fourteen times.

It would have been unusual in the so-called Scholastic period, which reached its peak in the thirteenth century, when Saint Thomas was writing, if any theologian or philosopher of that era had not relied on the same three groups of sources that Thomas himself did. We can take it for granted that in Thomas's time the Bible would have been the prime authority, just as it had been from earliest Christianity and would be until the Reformation and beyond. The pagan Greeks and Romans, too, depending of course on the topic that they were addressing, enjoyed a great deal of credibility among Christian writers; their influence is clear even when they are not cited by name. It is hard to imagine what the first few centuries of Christian literature would have been like had it not had recourse to Plato and Plotinus and Virgil and Cicero, to mention some of the most obvious.

The third group of authorities, the church fathers (so called since the earliest writers and teachers were almost exclusively men), were the church's first non-scriptural writers and teachers. The patristic period ("patristic" is related to the Greek and Latin words for "father") is usually said to range from the very end of the first century to near the middle of the seventh century in the Latin-speaking West and the middle of the eighth in the Greek-speaking East.

The fathers used both the Scriptures and the pagan authors as a basis for discussing the moral life. From the latter they retained what they considered advantageous and rejected what was antithetical to their understanding of Christian morality; the contributions of Stoic philosophy, which was popular at the time, were particularly beneficial in this regard. Some of the more speculative aspects of pagan philosophy and its terminology were useful in the fathers' attempts to understand and clarify teachings that were presented in the Scriptures, particularly in the New Testament, in a rudimentary way, such as those concerning the Trinity and the nature of the human and the divine in Christ. For some other Christian doctrines, however, like many of those having to do with the church and with grace and its ramifications, the Scriptures alone were the fathers' obligatory source.

By the fourth and fifth centuries, a number of fathers previous to that time, and some even in their own lifetimes, had acquired a reputation for orthodox teaching that covered them with the mantle of authority. At the end of the fourth century, Saint Jerome, who counted as an authoritative personality himself, put together a somewhat scattered catalogue of authors entitled *On Illustrious Men*, which helped to establish the reputations of numerous early Christian figures. It included, however, not only orthodox

Christians (many of whom we would now consider fathers, even if Jerome himself did not use that term), but also a few heretics and even some pagans.

Among the orthodox Christians whom Jerome did *not* mention was Augustine of Hippo, who was only starting his career when Jerome was writing *On Illustrious Men*. Not long after his death in 430, Augustine was seen as the greatest of the Latin fathers for both the profundity of his thought and the extensiveness of his writings, which touched upon almost every aspect of theology and Christian life. Ranked just below Augustine in the eyes of many were his contemporaries, Jerome and Ambrose of Milan, to whom was later added Gregory the Great, who died in 604. The reputation of these four fathers, and of others too many to mention by name in both the Latin West and the Greek East, was such that their writings had to be treated with the greatest respect. The respect for tradition that typified intellectual culture before the Age of Enlightenment in the eighteenth century helped to ensure that this would be so.

What the fathers said in their books and homilies was viewed very much in the same way that Scripture itself was viewed; indeed, insofar as they were the first Christians to comment on Scripture, the Bible was read in the way that the fathers themselves read and interpreted it. The Bible, to be sure, was always the prime text, but it was largely understood as the fathers understood it.

It is no surprise that the reverence and respect for the fathers that was part of the church's heritage was wholly shared by Saint Thomas, despite the fact that there are some notable differences between the fathers in general, on the one hand, and Thomas and his fellow Scholastics on the other. At the risk of oversimplifying, it could be said, for example, that the fathers were more pastoral and Thomas more academic, that the fathers relied more heavily on allegory than Thomas did, that the fathers were more diffuse and digressive and Thomas more analytic and systematic, that the fathers were more personal and Thomas more impersonal. Augustine in particular was different from Thomas in both disposition and theological approach. Yet Thomas's use of the fathers, and especially of Augustine, is marked by a serene continuity rather than by an emphasis on any kind of discontinuity.

Thomas's letter *De Sortibus* is not the sort of writing where one would expect to see differences aired and argued over. It briefly but comprehensively discusses a moral question of secondary importance, namely, whether and in what circumstances the use of lots should be allowed, albeit with possibly significant consequences. In the fourteen instances in which ancient Christian writers are referred to, Augustine is cited ten times, Bede twice (some would argue that Bede, having died in 735, lived at too late a period in the West to be counted among the fathers), Ambrose once, and Dionysius, the so-called "Areopagite," once.

In this brief work, Thomas uses the fathers to support his own views, as when he cites Augustine approvingly with regard to the influence that certain stars might have on human activity, and again, citing Augustine, when he condemns the workings of the occult in divinization. When both Augustine, in certain circumstances, and Ambrose seem to find the use of lots acceptable, Thomas nuances their position with a quotation from Bede's *Commentary on the Acts of the Apostles*. Thomas even uses one of his venerable predecessors to make a point in an amusing way, when he mentions a passage from the treatise *On Christian Doctrine* where Augustine employs the example of a mouse chewing one's clothing and whether or not this should be seen as an omen.

We in our day would almost certainly have felt the need to underline differences and discrepancies among the fathers whom Thomas cites, or could have cited in a more prolonged study. That would have been consistent with the contemporary idea of insisting that authorities validate themselves before they be accepted as authorities. But there is nothing like that in this little work from more than seven centuries ago. For an illustration of the same on a vastly bigger scale, one could go to the monumental *Summa theologiae*. All in all, *A Letter to a Friend about the Casting of Lots* is a kind of illustration in miniature of Thomas's use of and respect for the fathers.

6

Reliance on the Holy Spirit

Tobias Haller

After his encyclopedic inquiry into lots and their use, Thomas Aquinas finally addresses his friend's inquiry—whether lots may be used to elect a bishop. After lengthy investigation, his concise judgment is, "No."

Thomas notes, "this is a decision the Holy Spirit makes. . . . [I]n elections of this kind, it is unlawful for the lot to be used."

While Thomas allows for the limited use of lots to make some determinations, he deprecates lots as a means to render this decision.

Thomas, his nimble mind no doubt aware of the lurking objection around the corner—that this negative judgment seems to be contrary to the way the eleven filled the portion and share (the "lot") forsaken by Judas—has a *sed contra* at the ready.

Following the train of an argument by the Venerable Bede in his *Commentary on the Acts of the Apostles*, Thomas neatly turns the objection into support for his argument against any reliance on lots for filling episcopal vacancies: Pentecost makes all the difference.

Thomas notes that when the apostles cast lots to determine Judas's successor, though they gathered in prayer and invoked divine aid, they had not yet been enlightened and empowered by the Spirit. When time came for them to appoint the first deacons, they did not resort to lots, but drew on their Pentecostal charismata to make their decisions. Therefore, after Pentecost, the church should answer spiritual questions by spiritual means; divine power will provide divine answers. Q.E.D.

Thomas follows Bede in citing the selection of the first deacons as examples of the post-Pentecost authority of the apostles, and it fits in well with the dilemma caused by the deadlocked election in Vercelli.

A more telling example might be the confidence with which the apostles render their decision concerning what, if any, burden is to be placed upon gentile converts to the Christian faith. This decision is reached in the meeting of the apostolic council in Acts 15:28, which includes the confident assertion, "it has seemed good to the Holy Spirit and to us." Here we see the apostles "name it and claim it." As Bede comments, "That is, it has pleased the Holy Spirit, who, appearing as the arbiter of his own powers, *breathes where he wills*, and speaks the things which he wishes. And it has pleased us, not in accordance with our own will alone, but by virtue of the prompting of the same Spirit."

In this, as in all else, God reigns as First Cause, the unmoved mover of that which is moved. This raises the question, dear to Thomas's heart, of *causality*.

As Thomas notes at the end of his first chapter that "we look for information coming from lots about areas of human affairs, those that in some way have to do with us and that through our own efforts we can't know the answer to or bring about."

He examines how lots get their power in chapter IV. He rejects the notion of pure chance—because such a notion "limits divine providence, which is infinite." He also hints of his eventual finding on the case at hand, asserting that where divine rule is most evident, it is all the more unseemly to reject it.

The distinction is not only between operations depending on chance and operations depending on inspired reason, but also Thomas wants to stress that God orders all things well, and that divine aid is always available to the church.

While it might be tempting to resort to lots, Thomas suggests at a number of points who the Tempter might be, and he offers several warnings about the possible interference of unwelcome "spirits"—stressing that it is by prayer and reliance on religious covenant, rather than chance, that even decisions by lot must be made.

To resort to chance operations as a way of "leaving it up to God," not only risks putting God "to the test," but also leaves the God-given faculties of reason and spiritual discernment out of consideration.

As Thomas says, the Spirit "instructs human consciousness" in coming to the right decision. To forsake or neglect such instruction is irresponsible—at least when the humans making the decisions are open to God's will through the Spirit. Ultimately, people are responsible to make use of their God-given gifts in making determinations for the good of the people of God.

7

Richard Hooker and Thomas Aquinas

Matthew Fox

There lies a special and explicit relationship between Thomas Aquinas and the Anglican tradition by way of Richard Hooker (1554–1600), probably the most influential early Anglican theologian. He is often credited with laying down an attitude of deep respect for reason, tolerance, and the value of tradition.

Hooker respected Aquinas and in many ways tried to emulate him, including an attempt at writing a summa himself. I think that one reason the Anglican church did not succumb to the world-hating fundamentalism of some Protestant traditions is that Hooker—and by extension Aquinas—was too grounded in a love of creation to allow that to happen.

Both Hooker and Aquinas were also grounded in a deep understanding and appreciation of the work of the Holy Spirit in human affairs—and this, as I pointed out in my previous essay in this book—lies at the heart of the conclusion Aquinas came to in *De Sortibus*. We'll consider Hooker on the role of the Holy Spirit in human affairs, but first, to appreciate his perspective, we need to consider his teaching on panentheism and the indwelling of

Divinity in the human by way of the Father/Creator and the Son. That allows us to contextualize his teachings on the role of the Holy Spirit in human work.

Both Hooker and Aquinas share a common commitment to cosmology, that is, looking at the world as a whole and not isolating humans apart from the rest of nature. Both men, though deeply Christian, incorporate the pagan scientist Aristotle into their theology. Aquinas was condemned posthumously for following Aristotle's teaching on the consubstantiality of body and soul; and Hooker was denounced by the Puritan fundamentalists of his day, who accused him of being "another Aristotle."

Aquinas, who consciously chose to follow Aristotle rather than Plato, and wrote twelve books on Aristotle and not a single one on Plato, tells us he did so because Aristotle does not denigrate matter. To Aquinas, to know creation is to know God, for "Revelation comes in two volumes: Nature and the Bible" and "errors about creation will result in errors about God as well."

Hooker thought likewise when he said in his *Laws of Ecclesiastical Polity* he would "proceed to a consideration of the law, first of nature, then of Scriptures." Why? Because "the light of nature is a necessary background for the understanding of Holy Scripture, [and] the light of nature is not sufficient for our everlasting felicity, nor is Scripture alone sufficient for it."

Indeed, he takes on the fundamentalists of his day, the Puritans, with this charge: "God must be glorified in all things. . . . [I]t is their [the Puritans] error to think that the only law which God has appointed unto man in that behalf is the sacred Scriptures. By that which we work naturally, as when we breathe, sleep, move, we show for the glory of God as natural agents do . . . ."

There is a presence of God at work in all beings and all of creation in both Hooker's and Aquinas's view of the world. Hooker states: "Everything that God has made has something of God in it; and God has something of that in himself. . . . Everything, therefore, partakes of God—everything is his offspring and he influences them all." It is right to call this "the general indwelling of God in the creatures, and the creatures in him."

Aquinas speaks of the presence of God in all things by way of the divine power; the divine presence; and the divine essence, causing their being to exist. For Hooker, God is "omnipresent" and it is "impossible for God to withdraw his presence from anything," Aquinas agrees, "God must be everywhere and in all things. . . . Since God is everywhere, God is with all who are anywhere."

The Father and the Son dwell in us and we in them (both Hooker and Aquinas are panentheists). But the Spirit indwells as well—and here we come directly to Aquinas's *De Sortibus*. For as close as the Father and Son are to us, says Hooker, "The Spirit . . . [is] the nearest to us."

An amazing theology of the Spirit is celebrated here, and here the indwelling of the Trinity becomes complete: We in God and God in us in all the divine energy at work. The divine life is at work in us and our work. "This new life is like all other gifts and benefits that come from God; it comes from the Father, and only from the Father, but by way of the Son, and only by way of the Son, but through the Spirit and only through the Spirit." Says Aquinas: we are "co-creators with God."

Desire, according to Hooker, beckons all beings toward the Godhead and "leads to nothing less than the participation in God himself." Thus, all things seek God—"everything in the world may be said in some way or other to seek the highest, who is God himself." Aquinas had the same insight when he said: "There exists a natural friendship with God according to which anything whatsoever, insofar as it exists, seeks God and desires God as the first cause and the highest good and its own end."

For Hooker, as for Aquinas, culture and service of the community constitute an all-important matrix in which spirituality thrives and the Spirit roams and assists our work. This is at the heart of Aquinas's rejection of the use of lots as a way to choose a bishop in his letter: That humans must take seriously their powers of freedom, choice, and responsibility. The Holy Spirit works through human decision-making and courage, truth-seeking and truth-telling, and we are wise to leave the door open for Spirit to assist.

8

Aquinas as Anglican

CHRISTOPHER WELLS

Hailing from an influential family in southern Italy, Thomas Aquinas encountered Aristotle and broad, inter-cultural currents in Naples, from age thirteen, which led to his joining the nascent Dominican Order at age eighteen.

For the next thirty years, until his untimely death at age forty-nine, Aquinas studied and taught theology, mostly at universities in Paris and Rome, in which he rose to prominence as a great scholar, teacher, and faithful servant of the church. He did not speak English, or Middle English, and he never traveled to England. He would, however, have known of the English people, and of England as the place to which the great missionary-evangelist Saint Augustine of Canterbury was sent by Pope Gregory in 597.

Thomas also knew well the writings of Saint Anselm of Canterbury, the scholar-archbishop of the twelfth century, and of the early English Benedictine known as the Venerable Bede, both of whom contributed influentially to the first flowering of medieval theology, upon which foundation Aquinas built in his time. How, therefore, could Thomas Aquinas possibly have been an Anglican?

As a historical fact, he wasn't. And yet Anglicans have read, appropriated, and imitated Aquinas as a Common Doctor—one of his nicknames—since the major reformation within the English church in the sixteenth century, and many Anglican teachers, including the immensely influential Richard Hooker (1554–1600), have suggested there is something "Thomistic" about the Anglican theological and spiritual tradition. By this, we have meant that the spirit of Saint Thomas animates Anglican thinking and praying at its best, even when we have remained unaware of the debt.

I was taught this at seminary right from the start—sitting in the classroom of a devout Episcopalian at Yale Divinity School, who taught a seminar on Aquinas, not as a "Roman Catholic" theologian per se, but rather a broadly catholic theologian whom all Christians may share, whose thinking is marked by a salutary breadth, generosity of spirit, and ecumenical sensibility.

Living as he did almost three hundred years before the sixteenth-century Reformation, Aquinas was of course not a Protestant, but neither was he anti-Protestant. In the context of the western half of Christendom in which he worked he was pre-denominational. He knew just one church and devoted his life to the service of "one Lord, one faith, one baptism, one God and Father of all" (Ephesians 4:5–6), even as that commitment called forth from him a synthesizing of the Eastern, Greek-speaking part of the Christian world and the Western, Latin part.

Increasingly over the course of his short career, Aquinas sought to find common ground and to defend plurality wherever possible, drawing upon Latin and Greek sources in a bid to comprehend the whole of Christian teaching, and also to learn from non-Christians—Jews, Muslims, and ancient pagans—on the grounds that all truth is one, wherever it may be found.

Aquinas's whole body of work may be characterized as scriptural, traditionary, and reasonable. It is *scriptural*, since Thomas makes clear that Holy Scripture is the principal source and authority for Christian theology. It is *traditionary* as it labors to gather all the essentials of early church and catholic teaching, East and West, so that nothing may be lost. It is *reasonable* in that philosophy, and consequent argument, occupy a particular place in theology on pedagogical grounds, so that truth in its fullness may be uncovered, understood, and defended.

Thomas famously puts these three together in the programmatic first question of his greatest work, the *Summa theologiae*, when he says that Scripture is the first, "proper and necessary" authority in Christian theology, followed by the doctors of the church, who are "proper but only probable," and philosophy, which is "extrinsic and only probable." All three have their place by divine design, to accommodate human needs after the fall.

As Thomas insists, God *reveals* to human beings what they need to know for their salvation because they could not have discovered it on their own by "natural reason." These saving truths, given in Scripture and summarized in the creeds of the church, constitute a *wisdom* that mirrors God's own knowing, which is one and comprehends all things. Because everything exists thanks to God's gracious creating, Christian theology rightly imitates God by tending reverently and respectfully to all that God has made, and in this way shows forth the unity of truth. In a famous phrase, "grace does not destroy nature but perfects it."

Thomas's wonderful letter to his friend about the casting of lots, *De Sortibus*, displays this methodology perfectly. In a spirit of broad-minded, guileless generosity—Thomas always means what he says and seeks to be straightforward and fair—he takes three chapters to set out the question and consider it from all angles. Philosophical and scriptural authorities are marshaled mostly in a "natural" idiom to establish common touchstones concerning the operation of the human intellect and will and to propose a typology of lots (distributive, advisory, divining). In chapter IV, Thomas starts to draw conclusions and we glimpse something of his teacherly mastery as he places the philosophical foundation into an explicitly theological context; for "[God's] divine wisdom causes all things to exist . . . directing all to their appointed end . . . ."

On the appearance of God as principal actor, Thomas is able to organize a host of scriptural and traditional authorities to show that "human affairs aren't totally subject to human arrangements, but to a divine disposition," namely, providence—a major marker of Thomas's mature theology. Within this frame, the casting of lots may have its place as a seeking of divine judgment, under certain conditions: God should not be tested; "due reverence and devotion" must be observed; the matter should be sufficiently serious, not just "worldly"; and, critically, "divine inspiration" ought not be curtailed, which means for Thomas that lots are unlawful in the case of ecclesial elections. As Thomas writes, "it would be an injury towards the Holy Spirit, who instructs human consciousness so that it judges correctly," in keeping with Saint Paul's saying in 1 Corinthians 2:15, that "a spiritual person judges all things."

Anglicans—and many Christians—may find here an admirable balance and restraint, fed by theological seriousness, that is, a focus on *God*. Archbishop of Canterbury Geoffrey Fisher memorably said that Anglicans "have no doctrine of our own—we only possess the Catholic doctrine of the Catholic Church enshrined in the Catholic creeds."

To be sure, Anglican *life* looks different, in some ways, from that of our Roman Catholic, Orthodox, and Protestant colleagues. In division, we have all had to make decisions about how best to order our churches and account for various voices, recognizing, as well, the need for continual reform. But Anglicans have generally resisted developing new doctrines of our own, in recognition of the fact that we are not the whole—or one or true—church, but a *part* of it.

From the start, and more so as time went on, Anglicans have maintained a lively sense of loyalty to, and love of, all sides of the conflict out of which we were born. Speaking both Protestant and Catholic, as it were, we have sought to serve consensus in the tradition of Aquinas. His preference for Scripture above all, his steadfast insistence upon divine initiative, and his placing of God the Trinity and Jesus Christ at the center of Christian theology have resonated with our reformed heritage.

By the same token, Thomas's continual dependence on the early church writers, his robust account of all the sacraments (with baptism and Eucharist taken as "principal"), and his interest in councils as means of consensus have made sense to us in a catholic and ecumenical key.

In this conception, Christian theology seeks moderation not for its own sake but with a view both to fairness *and* synthesis: wise sifting in service of unity, conscious of "the immense responsibility . . . to maintain unshaken those common traditions that we have inherited," as Archbishop Fisher put it.

Common traditions, incorporating of course common prayer. With other Christians, Episcopalians mark the Feast Day of Saint Thomas on January 28 each year. Here, too, and most basically, we turn to our brother Thomas as a *Common* Doctor.

Thomas Aquinas: *pray for us.*

Appendix 1

A Review of Aquinas's Life and Principal Works

In many ways the life and work of the medieval philosopher and theologian Thomas Aquinas (1225–74) was not very exciting. He performed no miracles during his lifetime, nor did he make his reputation as a great orator, although we know that he preached very well.

Rather, he only did what Dominicans do: he studied, he prayed, he taught, he wrote a lot of both long and short works, and he preached and traveled to the places where his Order sent him. All standard fare for any Dominican. What sets Aquinas apart from every other Dominican was the fact that he did all these things extraordinarily well.

He was first and foremost a deeply religious man. Toward the end of his life, in 1273, after he had said Mass one day, Thomas was observed by the sacristan of the Church of San Domenico Maggiore in Naples gazing transfixed before an icon of the crucified Christ. The sacristan reported that he heard Christ speak to Thomas, saying, "You have written well of me, Thomas. What reward would you have for your labor?" Thomas replied, "Nothing but you, O Lord." Shortly after this one (and perhaps only) mystical experience, Thomas ceased writing altogether, declaring that his work was "nothing but straw."

Before he stopped writing, his output was staggering. The Dominican scholar and computer scientist Timothy McDermott estimates that Aquinas wrote eight and a half million words!

To get some sense of how relentlessly Thomas must have labored, it is enough to realize that he died at the young age of forty-nine, having been a Dominican for less than thirty of those years, and yet in that short time he produced about one hundred separate works.

The works of Thomas Aquinas can be grouped into about seven general categories, although others cluster his works in various different ways. The way I have done so is sufficient for the purpose of showing the exceptional range of his interests.

1. *Disputations:* First, the systematic disputations, which were debates open only to experts. There were also the quodlibital disputations, which were debates open to the public.

2. *Commentaries:* These were his insights into the works of the Greek philosophers, mostly Aristotle.

3. *Opuscula, or short works:* These were shorter or minor works, five of which were polemical works, five of which were expert opinions, and fifteen were letters on various subjects. This last category would include *De Sortibus.*

4. *Collections:* The longest and richest of these was the *Catena Aurea (The Golden Chain)*, an enormous collection of glosses from the early church writers and the Bible.

5. *Systematic works:* These were Thomas's greatest and longest works. They were meant to be comprehensive textbooks for the study of theology. They include the *Summa theologiae*, the *Summa Contra Gentiles*, and his *Commentary on the Sentences of Peter Lombard.* Throughout history, these works have had the greatest impact, and they are the ones Aquinas is most remembered for.

6. *Biblical commentaries:* Thomas wrote commentaries on Job, Psalms, Isaiah, Canticles, Jeremiah, as well as on Matthew and the Epistles of Paul. He completed nine in all.

7. *Mystical and liturgical works:* These should not be overlooked because of the insight they give us into the spiritual life of Aquinas. They include his sermons, as well as his commentaries on the Lord's Prayer and the Hail Mary, and also his great liturgical works, especially the *Office of Corpus Christi.*

Thomas's main insights were drawn from the Bible, the early writers of the church, and the Greek philosophers, especially from Aristotle. By basing himself primarily on Aristotle and particularly on Aristotle's theories of analogy, metaphysics, and ethics, Aquinas argued in all his works that there is no intrinsic conflict between faith and reason. In fact, he taught that they are intimately connected.

What is the key idea in Thomas Aquinas? Is it even possible to look at his massive output on such a wide variety of subjects and single out one, or even a few, central ideas? Certainly, it would be difficult to do that, although many scholars over the centuries have tried.

In any case, I think that virtually everyone would agree with the English philosopher Sir Anthony Kenny, who has called Thomas "one of the dozen greatest philosophers of the western world." I would add, "and one of the greatest theologians of the western world as well."

But this is to beg the question. *Why* is Aquinas among these great thinkers? Or do we even dare to ask that question?

I will try to have a go at it. It is because of what Aquinas was *not* as much as what he *was*. I believe that if Thomas Aquinas were alive today, he would emphatically *not* be a fundamentalist.

For me, the central idea of Aquinas is that human reason and divine faith are not in conflict, and that even though each is intimately related to the other, each has its own validity and its own value; each its own meaning and sphere. That idea is captured in a single famous phrase of Thomas Aquinas's, and that phrase is this: "grace does not destroy nature but perfects it." Or, in Latin, *gratia non tollit naturam, sed perficit.*

This idea is expressed in the very first section of Thomas's masterpiece, the *Summa theologiae:* "Since therefore grace does not destroy nature but perfects it," he wrote, "natural reason should minister to faith as the natural bent of the will ministers to charity" (I, I, 8, ad2).

As both a philosopher and a theologian, Aquinas's key idea about grace and nature are on full display in the letter translated in this book—*De Sortibus,* which means *"about the casting of lots,"* or as I call my translation, *A Letter to a Friend about the Casting of Lots.*

Thomas Aquinas's importance is not confined merely to Roman Catholics. (Nor is he the only focus of the religious order to which he belonged, although the Dominican Order—the Order of Preachers—must certainly be given credit for having carried out unsurpassed scholarship to reveal the insights of their most brilliant son and brother.) Thomas's relevance extends far wider. He is often called the "Common Doctor," meaning that he belongs to everyone who will take the time and make the effort to read his works.

Aquinas's works often cover unusual and yet still pertinent subjects, like the casting of lots; subjects that are still very much alive today. That is one of the reasons why Thomas is not just another figure from history.

At the end of the day Thomas Aquinas belongs to us all, and it is my hope that this interesting but mostly unknown work of a great saint and a great scholar, written during one of his most productive, fecund, and busy periods, will serve as a doorway to further interest in the Angelic Doctor.

What follows is a brief outline of Thomas's life and a listing of his principal works. Space demands that only his greatest and most famous works be included here.

But there is one exception in the chronology that follows, and that is the listing of the place and date of the writing of *De Sortibus* as well as the date and place where Thomas first met the person to whom his letter was later written. This is to help the reader to fix this *Letter to a Friend* into the larger picture of the life and work of the Angelic Doctor.

I have published this book for the Feast of Saint Thomas Aquinas, January 28, when both the Roman Catholic Church and the Anglican Communion remember the anniversary of Saint Thomas's death and celebrate the achievements of his life.

Appendix 2

Chronology

Some dates are approximate.

1224–25
Born at Roccasecca, near Aquino, midway between the Papal States and the Kingdom of Naples.

1231
Placed in the Abbey at Monte Casino.

1239
Goes to Naples to study. Comes into contact with Aristotle's works and first meets the Dominicans and is attracted to their lifestyle. Thomas asks to enter the Dominican Order.

1244
Sent to Rome by the Order but is detained for a year by his family in an effort to dissuade him from joining.

1245
Goes to Rome briefly and then to Paris, where he makes his novitiate and begins his studies. At this time, Paris was the intellectual center of Europe.

1248
Goes to Cologne with Albertus Magnus as his teacher. Albert was the leading intellectual of the Order at the time.

1250
Ordained a priest.

1252
Returns to Paris to pursue his undergraduate work. Writes his first great work, *Commentary on the Sentences of Peter Lombard*, the standard textbook of theology at the time. He also writes numerous other commentaries on Scripture and on Aristotle.

1256
Named a Master of Theology in Paris, the equivalent of today's PhD. Begins his second great work, the *Summa Contra Gentiles*. His fame as a great teacher and writer spreads.

1259
Returns briefly to Naples.

1260
Assigned to Orvieto at the request of Pope Urban VI to carry out various commissions for the Pope, including the *Office for Corpus Christi*. Also, he compiles *Catena Aurea* and completes the *Summa Contra Gentiles*. Meets and befriends James of Tonengo, to whom he later writes his letter entitled *De Sortibus*.

1268
Returns to Paris, where he begins his greatest and most famous work, the *Summa theologiae*.

1270–71
Writes *De Sortibus*, his letter to his friend on the casting of lots.

1272
Leaves Paris and returns to Naples to continue work on his *Summa theologiae*, which includes a short section on lots (Ia–IIae, Q95, art1–8).

1273
Ceases to write.

1274
Dies at forty-nine years old in the Cistercian Monastery of Fossanova on his way to the Council of Lyons.

1323
Declared a saint by Pope John XXII.

1567
Proclaimed a Doctor of the Church by the Dominican Pope Pius V.

For Further Reading

Chesterton, G. K. *St. Thomas Aquinas.* 1943. Reprint. Mansfield Centre, CT: Martino, 2011.

Davison, Andrew. *Participation in God: A Study in Christian Doctrine and Metaphysics.* Cambridge: Cambridge University Press, 2019.

Eardley, Peter S., and Carl N. Still. *Aquinas: A Guide for the Perplexed.* New York: Continuum, 2010.

Fox, Matthew. *Original Blessing: A Primer in Creation Spirituality.* New York: Tarcher/Putnam, 2000.

———. *Sheer Joy: Conversations with Thomas Aquinas on Creation Spirituality.* Mineola, NY: ixia, 2020.

———. *The Tao of Thomas Aquinas: Fierce Wisdom for Hard Times.* Bloomington, IN: iUniverse, 2020.

Kelly, J. N. D. *The Oxford Dictionary of Popes.* Oxford: Oxford University Press, 1986.

Kreeft, Peter. *Practical Theology: Spiritual Direction from Saint Thomas Aquinas.* San Francisco: Ignatius, 2014.

McDermott, Timothy. *Thomas Aquinas: Selected Philosophical Writings.* Selected and translated with an introduction and notes by Timothy McDermott. Oxford World's Classics. Oxford: Oxford University Press, 1993.

McInerny, Ralph. *Thomas Aquinas: Selected Writings.* Edited and translated with an introduction and notes by Ralph McInerny. London: Penguin, 1998.

O'Meara, Thomas. *Exploring Thomas Aquinas: Essays and Sermons.* Chicago: New Priory, 2017.

———. *Thomas Aquinas Theologian.* South Bend, IN: University of Notre Dame Press, 1997.

Pieper, Josef. *Guide to Thomas Aquinas.* Translated from the German by Richard and Clara Winston. San Francisco: Ignatius, 1962.

Porro, Pasquale. *Thomas Aquinas: A Historical and Philosophical Profile.* Translated by Joseph G. Tribbic and Roger W. Nutt. Washington, DC: Catholic University of America Press, 2016.

Appendix 2

Thomas Aquinas: Saint. *The Three Greatest Prayers. Commentaries on the Lord's Prayer, the Hail Mary, and the Apostles' Creed.* Translated into English by Laurence Shapcote. 1937. New edition with a foreword by Ralph McInerny. Manchester, NH: Sophia Institute, 1990.

Torrell, Jean-Pierre. *Saint Thomas Aquinas. Vol. 1 The Person and His Work. Vol. 2 Spiritual Master.* Translated by Robert Royal. Rev. ed. Washington, DC: Catholic University of America Press, 2003 and 2005.

Weisheipl, James A. *Friar Thomas D'Aquino: His Life, Thought and Works.* 1974. Reprint, Garden City, NJ: Doubleday, 1983.

CPSIA information can be obtained
at www.ICGtesting.com
Printed in the USA
FSHW011338310321
79962FS